JUST VISITING

JUST VISITING

*How Travel Has Enlightened Lives
and Viewpoints Throughout History*

GEORGE & KAREN GRANT

Cumberland House

NASHVILLE, TENNESSEE

Copyright © 1999 by George Grant and Karen Grant

Published by Cumberland House Publishing, Inc., 431 Harding Industrial Drive, Nashville, Tennessee 37211.

Jacket design by Tonya Presley
Text design by Bruce Gore, Gore Studio, Inc.

Library of Congress Cataloging-in-Publication Data

Grant, George, 1954–
    Just visiting : how travel has enlightened lives and viewpoints throughout
history / George & Karen Grant.
      p. cm.
    ISBN 1-58182-015-1 (pbk.)
    1. Europe--Description and travel. 2. Travelers--Europe--History.
I. Grant, Karen B., 1955–   . II. Title.
D90.G73   1999
914.04--dc21   99-14071
                                                               CIP

Printed in the United States of America
1 2 3 4 5 6 7 8 —04 03 02 01 00 99

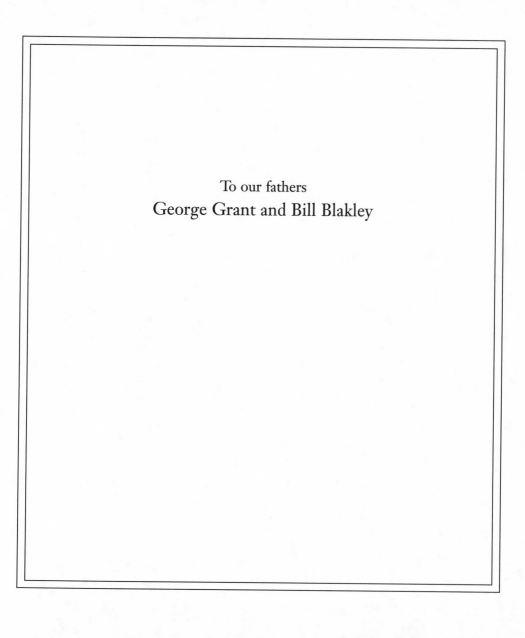

To our fathers
George Grant and Bill Blakley

CONTENTS

ACKNOWLEDGMENTS

Life is a movement and not a condition, a voyage and not a harbor.
ARNOLD TOYNBEE (1889–1975)

The contemporary Irish travel writer Frank Delaney once quipped, "One should know as much as possible about one's traveling companions. Do they smell? Do they drink? Are they punctual? Will they make you miss the train?" We have been privileged to travel through life with a whole host of dear friends, students, mentors, co-laborers, and family members who have displayed virtually none of those disagreeable traits which hamper progress or stymie joy along the way. As we have tramped about the world—and stumbled through the varied phases of our lives and careers—they have proven themselves to be happy traveling companions. The long and often difficult journeying has enabled us to know one another only too well—and still we desire to carry on. For that we are profoundly grateful.

Our fathers first gave us the taste and opportunity for travel. Going abroad was part of their job—but they made it a vital part of our experience and our worldview. Taking us from our narrow and protected existence in America's suburban geography of nowhere, they took us to Rome, Copenhagen, and Antwerp. They set us in the midst of the marvels of Paris, London, and Jerusalem. They gave us the world. Their irrepressible sense of adventure, their exuberant joy of discovery, and their purposeful personal sacrifice modeled for us more than they ever knew. This book is for them.

Ron and Julia Pitkin, both inveterate travelers, offered enthusiastic support for this project from its earliest gestation during a visit to the Scottish Highlands. We are grateful for their abiding friendship, constant encouragement, inquisitive appetites, substantive interest, and unflinching vision for publishing excellence.

Over the years we have had the opportunity to take several groups of travelers to visit many of the places profiled in this book. They happily endured the inevitable hardships of travel abroad while exulting in its many rewards. They unquestioningly followed us off the beaten path to discover dusty antiquarian bookshops, obscure historical sites, and quirky little pubs, out of the way sausage stands, or hole-in-the-wall falafel counters. They trudged through the countryside in sweltering heat, bitter cold, or torrential downpours, rode the rough roads in swaying or stultifying coaches, and trundled along in helter-skelter railcars with nary a complaint. Through it all they made our visits so much richer and enjoyable by their conversation, their friendship, and their desire to see more, know more, and discover more.

The soundtrack for this project was provided by the appropriately disparate music of William Coulter, The Baltimore Consort, Aine Minogue, The Anjali Quartet, Michael Card, and Aoife Ni Fhearraigh. The midnight musings were provided by the equally diverse prose of James Kunstler, William Hannah, Thomas Chalmers, Hilaire Belloc, Herman Melville, and Abraham Kuyper.

To all these, we offer our sincerest thanks.

Of course, our deepest debt in life is owed to our three beloved children, Joel, Joanna, and Jesse. They have been our dearest, surest, and best travel mates. It should come as no surprise then that they were our chief inspiration for this scrapbook of favorite people and places.

ADVENT 1998
King's Meadow Farm

INTRODUCTION

*Two roads diverged in a wood, and I—I took the one less traveled by, and that
has made all the difference.*
ROBERT FROST (1874–1963)

According to the Latin proverb, "Travelers may change their climate
but never their souls." While it may be admitted that this statement is
essentially true, there also can be little doubt that travelers may at least
change their thinking. Seeing the world—the different sights, sounds,
textures, hues, and passions of cultures different than their own—
affords travelers with a unique perspective that militates against prejudice, parochialism, and pettiness. As Mark Twain said, travel somehow
"broadens the mind and softens the heart." More often than not, travel
serves to sunder our uninformed native preconceptions and to establish
more mature perspectives.

For that reason, travel has always been a component part of a well
rounded education. The banal prejudice and narrow presumption that
inevitably accompany an unexposed, inexperienced, and undiscerning
existence can often be ameliorated only by the disclosure of the habits,
lifestyles, rituals, celebrations, and aspirations of the peoples beyond
the confines of our limited parochialism. The great Dutch patriot

Groen van Prinsterer aptly commented to his students, "See the world and you'll see it altogether differently."

As a result, in times past, travel was seen as far more significant than just fun and games. It was for more than mere rest and relaxation. It was intended to be more than simply a vacation or a getaway. Instead, it was a vital aspect of the refined instruction in art, music, literature, architecture, politics, business, science, and divinity. It was, according to Benjamin Franklin, "the laboratory where theory meets practice, where notion encounters application."

Travel has thus enlightened lives and perspectives throughout history. Some of the most famous books, some of the most influential perspectives, and some of the most remarkable social transformations have had their genesis in some great quest or expedition or journey or voyage—from Agamemnon in Troy and Caesar in Gaul to Marco Polo in China and Richard the Lionhearted in Outremer, from Christopher Columbus in the Caribbean and Cotton Mather in Massachusetts Bay to Charles Lindbergh in the Spirit of St. Louis and John Glenn in the Shuttle Enterprise. Just visiting has left an indelible mark upon the human experience.

This book is a celebration of a small sampling of the great cities of the world. It is also an exploration of how those cities have affected some of the brightest minds, clearest observers, greatest leaders, and best writers through the ages. It is both a recollection of some of our own visits and an investigation of some of theirs. It celebrates the joys, as well as the hazards—even some of the familiar or traditional meals—of the visiting life.

Admittedly this kind of book bears the inevitable stamp of subjective experience. In fact, it is the third in a series of books we've undertaken to exposit our very personal passions in life. *Letters Home* deals with the sage counsel of bygone days and *Best Friends* deals with the ways friendship shapes our lives. Yet to come are volumes on gardening, books, sports, food, and sundry lost causes. Thus, by its very nature, this book—like all the others in the series—is more a testimony than a documentary.

The vague idea for the project first began to come together following a long and lively conversation about the integration of education and visits abroad. Whilst warmly ensconced against the brisk Highland winds in a hospitable Scottish inn, we discussed the ways travel had changed us, our view of the world around us, and our expectations in the widely divergent arenas of politics, music, literature, cuisine, fashion, transportation, architectural design, gardening, and recreation. In other words, we talked of all the ways travel had changed our lives. We began to wonder about the ways that it had similarly changed others—we had an uninformed hunch that ours was not an entirely unique experience. So, we determined to inform our speculations. Over the next several years, in an on again, off again fashion, we made note of the effects of travel on the lives of the people we read or read about.

We were admittedly a little surprised—even though our informal research confirmed our suspicions. We were surprised because of the voluminous amount of material on the subject available to the modern reader—albeit scattered to the four winds. As a result, the most difficult task we faced in putting together this little book proved to be more a matter of what to leave out rather than what to include.

According to James Ferguson, the famed nineteenth century Scottish architect, "Travel is more than a visitor seeing sights; it is the profound changing—the deep and permanent changing—of that visitor's perspective of the world, and of his own place in it." That certainly has been the case in our lives—it is our prayer that this little book may help you discover that truth as well.

The Grand Tour

From the end of the fifteenth century to the beginning of the twentieth, it was expected that all members of high born families; aspiring artists, poets and historians; prospective members of the diplomatic corps; and young bon vivants would undertake an extended pilgrimage to the great cities of the Western world. It was considered an essential part of a well-rounded education. Indeed, in many elite circles, it was believed to be the capstone of a true classical curriculum. Many of the most eminent people in history thus set out on what became known as the Grand Tour just before they entered public life. Traveling to the great centers of culture, history, and influence, they sought to take in as much of the art, music, literature, architectural sites, historical monuments, social revelries, and culinary delights as they possibly could. Taking anywhere from just a few weeks to several months, the Grand Tour was intended to help the next generation of leaders to learn the languages, customs, and mores of far-flung lands and societies. They desired to broaden their horizons, test the practicality of their book learning, and to deepen their social and academic awareness. It was to enable them to eventually do all they were called to do and be all they were called to be.

The world is a book, and those who do not travel, read only a page.
ST. AUGUSTINE (354–430 A.D.)

The traveler sees what he sees, the tourist sees what he has come to see.
G. K. CHESTERTON (1874–1936)

Travel's greatest purpose is to replace an empty mind with an open one.
WILLIAM HAZLITT (1778–1830)

She had resolved that he should travel through
All European climes, by land or sea,
To mend his former morals, and get new,
Especially in France and Italy
At least this is the thing most people do.
LORD BYRON (1788–1824)

Before he sets out, the traveler must possess fixed interests and facilities to be served by travel.
→ GEORGE SANTAYANA (1863–1952) ←

A pilgrim is a traveler that is taken seriously.
→ AMBROSE BIERCE (1842–1914) ←

Own only what you can carry with you; know language, know countries, know people. Let your memory be your travel bag.
→ ALEKSANDER SOLZHENITSYN (1918–) ←

'Tis pleasant, through the loopholes of retreat,
to peep at such a world; to see the stir
of the great Babel, and not feel the crowd;
to hear the roar she sends through all her gates,
at a safe distance, where the dying sound
falls a soft murmur on the uninjured ear.
Thus sitting and surveying thus at ease
The globe and its concerns, I seem advanced
To some secure and more than mortal height,
That liberates and exempts me from them all.
It turns submitted to my view, turns round
With all its generations; I behold
The tumult, and am still. The sound of war
Has lost its terrors ere it reaches me;
Grieves, but alarms me not. I mourn the pride
And avarice that make man a wolf to man,
Hear the faint echo of those brazen throats,

By which he speaks the language of his heart,
And sigh, but never tremble at the sound.
He travels and expiates, as the bee
From flower to flower, so he from land to land:
The manners, customs, policy of all
Pay contribution to the store he gleans;
He sucks intelligence in every clime,
And spreads the honey of his deep research
At his return—a rich repast for me.
He travels, and I too. I tread his deck,
Ascend his topmast, through his peering eyes
Discover countries, with a kindred heart
Suffer his woes, and share in his escapes;
While fancy, like the finger of a clock,
Runs the great circuit, and is still at home.

꘠ WILLIAM COWPER (1731–1800) ꘠

He who would travel happily must travel light.
ANTOINE DE SAINT-EXUPERY (1900–1944)

Bad things happen to good people. Worse things happen at sea.
JOHN PAUL JONES (1747–1792)

A traveler must have the back of an ass to bear all, a tongue like the tail of a dog to flatter all, the mouth of a hog to eat what is set before him, the ear of a merchant to hear all and say nothing.
THOMAS NASHE (1567–1601)

Those who travel about England for their pleasure, or, for that matter, about any part of Western Europe, rightly associate with such travel the pleasure of history: for history adds to a man, giving to him, as it were, a great memory of things like a human memory, but stretched over a far longer space than that of one human life. It makes him, I do not say wise and great, but certainly in communion with wisdom and greatness. It adds also to the soil he treads, for to this it adds meaning. How good it is when you come out of Tewkesbury by the Cheltenham road, to look upon those fields to the left and know that they are not only pleasant meadows, but also the place in which the fate of English medieval monarchy was decided; or, as you stand by that ferry which is not known enough to Englishmen (for it is one of the most beautiful things in England) and look back and see Tewkesbury tower framed between tall trees over the level of the Severn, to see the Abbey buildings in your eye of the mind—a great mass of similar stone with the Norman walls, standing to the right of the building. All this historical sense and the desire to marry history with travel is very fruitful and nourishing.

⊰ HILAIRE BELLOC (1870–1953) ⊱

Do not lose your knowledge that man's proper estate is an upright posture, an intransigent mind, and a step that travels unlimited roads.

             ◦⟩ AYN RAND (1905–1982) ⟨◦

Returning he proclaims by many a grace,
By shrugs and strange contortions of his face,
How much a dunce that has been sent to roam
Excels a dunce that has been kept at home.

          ◦⟩ WILLIAM COWPER (1731–1800) ⟨◦

It is only fear that makes you travel.

       ◦⟩ ROBERT LEWIS STEVENSON (1850–1894) ⟨◦

It is only fear that makes you stay at home.

        ◦⟩ BONNIE PRINCE CHARLIE (1720–1788) ⟨◦

If you always go where you have always have gone and always do what you have always done, you will always be what you are now.

          ◦⟩ TRISTAN GYLBERD (1954–) ⟨◦

Cease to persuade, my loving Proteus;
Home-keeping youth have ever homely wits:
Were't not affection chains thy tender days
To the sweet glances of thy honored love,
I rather would entreat thy company
To see the wonders of the world abroad,
Than living dully sluggardized at home,
Wear out thy youth with shapeless idleness.

                           ❧ WILLIAM SHAKESPEARE (C. 1564–1616) ☙

With visions of redemption, I walk against the crowd.

                         ❧ ARTHUR QUILLER-COUCH (1863–1944) ☙

To a wise man all the world's his soil:
It is not Italy, nor France, nor Europe,
That must bound me,
If my fates call me forth.

                         ❧ BEN JOHNSON (1572–1637) ☙

Never forget that every place is unique—just like every place else.

                         ❧ TRISTAN GYLBERD (1954–) ☙

It is better to have traveled and gotten lost than to never have traveled at all.

of GEORGE SANTAYANA (1863–1952) ɵ

All is fair in love and war and travel abroad.

of H. L. MENCKEN (1880–1956) ɵ

There is nothing gives a man such spirits,
Leavening his blood as cayenne doth a curry,
As going at full speed—no matter where its
Direction be, so tis but in a hurry,
And merely for the sake of its own merits;
For the less cause there is for all this flurry
The greater is the pleasure in arriving
At the end of travel—which is the driving.

of LORD BYRON (1788–1824) ɵ

Education has produced a vast population able to read who are yet unable to distinguish what is worth reading. Likewise inexpensive packaged tours abroad have produced a vast number of sightseers who are yet unable to distinguish what sites are worth seeing.

of G. M. TREVELYAN (1876–1962) ɵ

Traveling abroad is a progressive exercise in the discovery of our own ignorance.

ᴥᵂᴵᴸᴸᴵᴬᴹ WILLIAM BLAKE (1757–1827) ᵂ

You can lead a youngster abroad, but you cannot make him travel.

ᴥ HILAIRE BELLOC (1870–1953) ᵂ

It appears that the rumor is in fact true: the world is run by C students.

ᴥ JEAN RENOIR (1894–1979) ᵂ

The man who, with undaunted toils
Sails unknown seas to unknown soils,
With various wonders feasts his sight:
What stranger wonders does he write.
We read and in descriptions view
Creatures which Adam never knew:
For when we risk no contradiction
It prompts the tongue to deal in fiction.

ᴥ JOHN GAY (1685–1732) ᵂ

To travel is to discover that everyone is wrong about the other countries.

ᴥ ALDOUS HUXLEY (1894–1963) ᵂ

Abroad, there are but two classes of travel: first and with children.
→ ROBERT BENCHLEY (1889–1945) ←

I never travel without a diary—one should always have something
sensational to read.
→ OSCAR WILDE (1854–1900) ←

Travel is a ceaseless fount of surface education, but its wisdom
Will be simply superficial, if thou add not thoughts to things.
→ FREDERICK JACKSON TURNER (1861–1932) ←

Ye distant spires, ye antique towers,
Hold me in thy sway;
Make me see, make me flee,
Unto thy rich array.
For there amidst, and there consist
The root and branch and leaf,
Of faith and hope and love persist
In this, the world of grief.
→ TRISTAN GYLBERD (1954–) ←

I want to go a'wandering about th'whole girth
So who, in mind, might now declare
That I, at all, should now suppress such mirth?
Or smother notions of such a dare?

Across the wide horizon to cities unknown
To visit monuments and hallowed halls
From whence this civilization's now grown
I'll venture forth where 'ere the Tour calls.

            JAMES STUART KILMANY (1866–1939)

THEODORE ROOSEVELT IN 1868

The long and varied history of the Grand Tour—which invariably began in London and ended in Rome with visits to Edinburgh, Paris, Venice, Florence, Vienna, Jerusalem, and innumerable other great cities along the way—includes amazing stories of such travelers as Queen Victoria, John Milton, John Ruskin, Percy Shelly, Anna Jameson, Lord Byron, Adam Smith, Thomas Hobbes, Elizabeth Barrett Browning, Joseph Addison, Charles Dickens, William Wordsworth, Emma Hamilton, William Thackery, and Edward Lear. And the Grand Tour was not merely an English phenomenon. Americans such as Washington Irving, Julia Ward Howe, Mark Twain, Henry Adams, Stephen Crane, Harriet Beecher Stowe, and Henry Cabot Lodge also traveled abroad as youngsters.

Among that eminent number was Theodore Roosevelt.

By any measure, Roosevelt turned out to be quite a remarkable man. Before his fiftieth birthday, he had served as a New York state legislator, the undersecretary of the Navy, police commissioner for the city of New York, U.S. civil service commissioner, the governor of the state of New York, the vice president under William McKinley, a colonel in the U.S. Army, and two terms as president of the United States. In addition, he had run a cattle ranch in the Dakota Territories, served as a reporter and editor for several journals, newspapers, and magazines, and conducted scientific expeditions on four continents. He read at least five books every week of his life and wrote nearly fifty on an astonishing array of subjects—from history and biography to natural science and social criticism. He enjoyed hunting, boxing, and wrestling. He was an amateur taxidermist, botanist, ornithologist, and astronomer. He was a devoted family man who lovingly raised six children. And he enjoyed a lifelong romance with his wife.

During his long and varied career he was hailed by supporters and rivals alike as the greatest man of the age—perhaps one of the greatest of all ages. According to Thomas Reed, speaker of the House of Representatives, Roosevelt was a "new-world Bismark and Cromwell combined." Indeed, according to President Grover Cleveland, he was "one of the ablest men yet produced in human history." Senator Henry Cabot Lodge asserted that, "Since Caesar, perhaps no one has attained among crowded duties and great responsibilities, such high proficiency in so many separate fields of activity." After an evening in his company, the epic poet Rudyard Kipling wrote, "I curled up on the seat opposite and listened and wondered until the universe seemed to be spinning round—and Roosevelt was the spinner." Great Britain's Lord Charnwood exclaimed, "No statesman for centuries has had his width of intellectual range; to be sure no intellectual has so touched the world with action." Even his lifelong political opponent, William Jennings Bryan, was bedazzled by his prowess. "Search the annals of history if you will," Bryan said.

"Never will you find a man more remarkable in every way than he."

Amazingly, as a youngster, Roosevelt showed little promise of his later greatness. He was born a sickly child on October 27, 1858. His father, Theodore Roosevelt Sr., was a sixth generation New York burgher—the scion of one of the richest and most influential old Dutch families of Manhattan. By all accounts, young Theodore displayed an exuberant, disciplined, and masculine joy of life. The child's mother, Martha Bulloch Roosevelt, was an unmistakable Southern belle—the beautiful and delicate daughter of one of the most prominent Scottish plantation families of Georgia.

Though the child was the heir of two proud traditions which he would cherish for the rest of his life—the sturdy Dutch industrial mercantilism of the North and the romantic Scottish pioneer agrarianism of the South—his fragile health was a matter of constant concern. He suffered from an unceasing barrage of ailments and conditions—all somewhat related to congenital asthma, which the family generically called cholera morbus. His little body was continually wracked by coughs, colds, nausea, and chronic diarrhea. His younger sister would later relate that, "Rarely, even at his best, could he sleep without being propped up in bed or a big chair." His gauntness and fragility reminded his mother of the pale withering azaleas of early summer. And it was whispered that he probably would not live to see his fourth birthday. He was often confined as an invalid for months at a time. And his earliest memories were of fitful nights gasping for a breath of air while both of his parents hovered over his sickbed.

During his long convalescences, he benefited from the tales and reminiscences of his parents and grandparents. They regaled him with stories, legends, and songs from the past. They filled his mind with florid romance, dashing adventure, and a fierce sense of his proud heritage that would ever after shape his consciousness. Later, he continued to feed his voracious appetite for such things, becoming a lifelong avid reader.

His father, concerned that Teddy's sickly body would never allow him to enjoy the kind of full life he constantly read about, at last confronted him with the issue. "Theodore," the big man said, "you have the mind but you have not the body. And without the body the mind cannot go as far as it should. You must make your body. It is hard drudgery to make one's body, but I know you will do it."

His mother later remembered that the boy's reaction was the half-grin, half-snarl which later became world famous. Jerking his head back, he set his jaw and replied, "I'll make my body. By heaven, I will." Indeed, he did. With bulldog tenacity, he began to make daily visits to a local gym to lift weights, to box and spar, and to compete in gymnastic exercises. Later, he installed a small gym in the second floor piazza just off his bedroom where he literally beat his body into submission.

In an attempt to strengthen his frail son's body all the more, the elder Roosevelt packed up his family each spring and summer and traveled to the rugged shores of Oyster Bay on Long Island. There Teddy and the other children began to appreciate the joys of nature. They swam along the beach, rode horses up and down the rolling hills, hiked through the woods, hunted in the meadows, fished in the streams, and rowed across the bay. They built wigwams at the edge of the forest, gathered hickory nuts and wild apples, climbed to the tops of the tallest trees, and scampered down long, leafy foot trails.

Despite his incessant illness, Teddy seemed to have an inexhaustible fund of energy. He could hardly be kept still—even when sorely afflicted by one of his debilitating asthma attacks. His many hours of enforced reading combined with his keen powers of observation in the woods quickly combined to make him something of a prodigy. He became a serious student of natural history—keeping detailed journals and notes of his sagacious studies of local flora and fauna. By the time he was seven, he had begun a little museum containing a carefully indexed and classified collection of insects, bird nests, rocks, minerals, and cocoons. And by the time he was nine, his repertoire of specimens had expanded to snakes, rodents, birds, and small mammals. He even began to learn the technical processes of taxidermy.

When the family embarked on a yearlong Grand Tour of Europe in 1869, Teddy's intellectual proclivities became particularly pro-nounced. He not only reveled in the art and architecture, history and pageantry, chivalry and nobility of the continent, he was fascinated by its spectacular natural beauty—from the dales of England to the forests of Germany, from the mountains of Switzerland to the valleys of the Rhine, from the highlands of Lombardy to the lowlands of Belgium—he was bedazzled by the infinite variety of creation.

His diaries indicate a mind capable of astonishingly prodigious recall and insatiable appetites. Already, historian Edmund Morris points out, the contours of his interests and character were in evidence: "Promptness, excitability, warmth, histrionics, love of plants and animals, physical vitality, dee-light, sensitivity to birdsong, fascination with military display, humor, family closeness, the conservationist, the historian, the hunter—all are here."

In addition to his marked intellectual growth, by the time the family returned home, Teddy's conscience was also pricked by the poverty and deprivation he had witnessed abroad. His father was either the founder or an early supporter of virtually every cultural, humanitarian, and philanthropic endeavor in the city of New York. His unceasing efforts to establish the New York Orthopedic Hospital, the Children's Aid Society, and the Newsboys' Lodging House had already made a deep impression on his son. He was instrumental in organizing the Protective War Claims Association, the Soldiers' Employment Bureau, and the Blackwell's Island Sanitarium Society. The founding meetings of the American Museum of Natural History and the Metropolitan Museum of Art were both called by Teddy's father and held in the family's front parlor. And he made certain that the life and fellowship of the Madison

Square Presbyterian Church were central priorities for them all—not just on Sundays when he taught a mission class, but throughout the week. As a result, young Teddy had a ready context within which to develop his newly awakened concerns.

Toward the end of 1872, the Roosevelts embarked on yet another foreign adventure—one even more adventurous than their previous Grand Tour of Europe. In addition to long sojourns in England, Germany, and Italy, they visited the Middle East—including Palestine, Syria, and Egypt. It was on this trip that all of the disparate aspects of Teddy's wide-ranging interests—books, history, scientific observation, the outdoor life, and Christian social concern—began to be fully integrated into a cohesive worldview. As his father related, "He went away a boy and returned a young man."

Later, Roosevelt would look back on his opportunity to go on the Grand Tour—not once, but twice—as one of the most formative events in his remarkably eventful life. "Travel abroad changed me altogether for the good," he wrote. "I was a sickly, delicate boy, suffered much from asthma, and frequently had to be taken away on trips to find a place where I could breathe. Even after I had defeated the ailments that assaulted my body, it was necessary that I be taken away on trips to find a place where I could think. The Grand Tour enabled me to grow beyond the stunted existence of my small experience."

And so it did.

An American Sendoff Meal

Such a feast we all had for our sendoff meal, I have never seen before or since; it was the essence of Southern hospitality at its very finest.

THEODORE ROOSEVELT (1858–1919)

Red Cabbage Slaw

1 lge. shredded head red cabbage, 1 lb. large coarsely grated carrots, 4 stripped celery stalks, 1/3 c fresh lemon juice, 1/4 c cider vinegar, 1/2 T mustard, 1 T celery seeds, salt and pepper to taste

In a large bowl, toss the vegetables. In a separate bowl, blend the lemon juice, vinegar, and mustard. Stirring continuously, add the oil and blend until just emulsified. Add the celery seeds and salt and pepper to taste. Pour over the vegetable mixture and toss well. Serve cold.

Southern Fried Chicken

1 lge. chicken, 1 qt. buttermilk, 2 T salt, 4 T oregano, 2 T black pepper, 5 T garlic powder, 4 c flour, shortening

Cut up and wash the chicken. Immerse the chicken in buttermilk in a bowl and let sit at least 2 hours, preferably overnight. In a large paper sack, mix the seasonings with flour. Heat 1 inch of shortening in a heavy cast iron skillet. Shake each piece of chicken in the paper sack, and when the shortening is very hot but not yet smoking place the chicken into the pan. Reduce the heat to medium. Turning only once, let the chicken cook 10 to 15 minutes per side until the outside is brown and crispy but the inside is still moist.

Pan Gravy

2 to 3 T fat from fried chicken, 2 to 3 T flour, milk, pepper to taste

Pour off all but 2 to 3 T fat after the chicken is fried, being careful to keep some of the "cracklings" left over from chicken. Add the flour to the fat mixture and stir over low heat until well browned. Slowly add milk at sides of skillet so that it heats as it is added, stirring all the while. Continue stirring, adding milk bit by bit until the gravy is the desired consistency. Add pepper to taste.

Mashed Potatoes

6 white potatoes, 4 T butter, 1/4 c milk, salt and pepper to taste, parsley to taste

Peel and quarter the potatoes. In a pan, boil for 20 to 30 minutes until tender. Drain water, stir in butter, milk, and seasonings. Mash until smooth and well blended. Serve with pan gravy.

Green Beans

2 lbs. green beans, 1 small chopped onion, 2 T butter, 1 gal. water, 1/4 lb. salt pork, butter and pepper to taste

Wash and string beans. In a cooking pot, sauté the onion in 2 T butter until translucent. Add water and bring to a boil. Add salt pork and beans. Lower heat to simmer and cook about 1 hour. Drain, add butter and pepper to taste.

Corn Pudding

5 ears corn, 4 slices bacon, 1 chopped yellow onion, 1/4 c cornmeal, 2 c milk, salt and pepper to taste, 3 eggs, beaten

Clean corn, scrape kernels along with milky liquid from the cob. Set aside. Fry bacon in a heavy pan. Remove bacon and sauté the onion in bacon grease. Add corn, cornmeal, milk, and seasonings. Stir until thickened. Remove pan from heat, stir in eggs. Cook in a medium oven (350°) 30 to 40 minutes until set and browned on top.

Hot Fruit Compote

4 peeled and sliced peaches, 4 peeled and sliced pears, 1/2 lb. dried prunes, 1/2 lb. dried apricots, 1 c raisins, 1/4 c brandy, 1 c pecans or walnuts, 1 t cinnamon, 1/2 t nutmeg, 1/2 c sugar, juice of half a lemon, 1/4 c butter

Soak fruit overnight in brandy. In a baking dish, alternate layers of fruit with nuts, sprinkling each layer with cinnamon/nutmeg/sugar mixture. Drizzle lemon juice over the compote and dot with butter. Bake in a medium oven (350°) for 30 to 40 minutes.

Sponge Cake with Sugarcreme

4 large eggs, 1¼ c sugar, 2 c cake flour, 2 t baking powder, 1 c hot milk infused with vanilla bean, 6 T soft unsalted butter, 1½ c brown sugar, ½ c sugar, ¼ c unsalted butter, ½ c heavy cream infused with vanilla bean

Grease and flour a 9" x 13" cake pan. In a bowl, beat the eggs and ¼ c sugar well. In a separate bowl, sift together the cake flour, baking powder, and salt and beat into the egg and sugar mixture. Add the milk and 6 T butter, and stir vigorously until combined well. Pour the batter into the prepared cake pan and bake in a medium oven (350°) for about 1 hour. Cool.

Combine 1½ c brown sugar, ½ c sugar, ¼ c butter, and cream in a saucepan and bring to a boil. Stirring constantly, bring the mixture to the soft ball stage. Remove immediately from the heat and cool. Stir the sugarcreme until it becomes spreadable. Pour it over the sponge cake and let cool.

London

T hough London was for more than a century the most populous city on earth, it was also always a collection of villages. Each village used to have a unique quality and some still do. The government focuses on Whitehall, with power derived from Parliament in Westminster—incomplete without the royal family, whose public and private life is still centered around St. James' Park. Newspapers used to be in Fleet Street, book publishers in Bloomsbury, films in Wardour Street, theatres in Shaftesbury Avenue, fashion in Mayfair and fruit and vegetables in Covent Garden.

Here is the place where England ends—and here is where England
can begin.

ᴏᶀ G. K. CHESTERTON (1874–1936) ᶀᴏ

As I came down the Highgate Hill
I met the sun's bravado,
And saw below me, fold on fold,
Grey to pearl and pearl to gold,
This London like a land of old,
The land of Eldorado.

ᴏᶀ HENRY HOWARTH BASHFORD (1880–1962) ᶀᴏ

Oh, London is a man's town,
There's power in the air.

ᴏᶀ HENRY VAN DYKE (1853–1933) ᶀᴏ

Oh London Town's a fine town,
And London sights are rare,
And London ale is right ale
And brisk's the London air.

ᴏᶀ JOHN MASEFIELD (1874–1951) ᶀᴏ

The mighty fleet of Wren, with their topgallants and mainsails of stone. The nautical simile leaps to the mind at the sight of Wren's white spires and towers, and it is appropriate, too, to the material in which Wren worked. Portland stone is a marine deposit of the Jurassic period before Britain first at Heaven's command arose from out the azure main. Its beds are full of fossils of marine creatures, cockles, sea urchins, starfish, and oysters. You can see shell imprints on the freshly cut whitbed stone on the top of the new Bush building, and you can see the horses' heads—as certain sea fossils are called by masons—on the weathered parapet of St. Paul's. You can see and feel the shells projecting from the plinth of King Charles' statue at Charing Cross. It is a strange thought that the majesty of the capital of this sea-joined empire should come itself from beneath the sea. How could the poets have missed such a theme?

ᵉᵗ JAMES BONE (1872–1946) ᵗᵉ

By Charing Cross in London Town
There runs a road of high renown,
Where antique books are ranged on shelves
As dark and dusty as themselves.
And many book lovers have spent
Their substance there with great content,
And vexed their wives and filled their homes
With faded prints and massive tomes.

               NORMAN DAVEY (1888–1959)

A livid sky on London
And like the iron steeds that rear
A shock of engines halted,
And I knew the end was near:

And something said that far away, over the hills and far away,
There came a crawling thunder and the end of all things here.
For London Bridge is broken down, broken down, broken down,
As digging lets the daylight on the sunken streets of yore,
The lightning looked on London town, the broken bridge of
London town,
The ending of a broken road where men shall go no more.

I saw the kings of London town,
The kings that buy and sell,
That built it up with penny loaves
And penny lies as well:

And where the streets were paved with gold the shriveled paper
shone for gold,
The scorching light of promises that pave the streets of hell.
For penny loaves will melt away, melt away, melt away,
Mock the mean that haggled in the grain they did not grow;
With hungry faces in the gate, a hundred thousand in the gate,
A thunder flash in London and the finding of the foe.

         ⊰ G. K. CHESTERTON (1874–1936) ⊱

This royal throne of kings,
This sceptered isle,
This earth of majesty, this seat of Mars,
This other Eden, this demi-paradise,
This fortress built by nature herself
Against infection and the hand of war,
This happy breed of men, this little world.
This precious stone set in the silver sea,
Which serves it in the office of a wall,
Or as a moat defensive to a house
Against the envy of less happier lands;
This blessed plot, this earth, this realm,
This England.
Renowned for deeds as far from home
For Christian service and true chivalry
As unto the Holy Sepulchre itself, this land
Of such dear souls, this dear, dear land:
This England.

꘍ WILLIAM SHAKESPEARE (C. 1564–1616) ꘍

Forget six counties overhung with smoke,
Forget the snorting steam and piston stroke,
Forget the spreading of the hideous town;
Think rather of the pack-horse on the down,
And dream of London, small, and white, and clean.

WILLIAM MORRIS (1834–1896)

Though grief and fondness in my breast rebel
When injured Thales bids the town farewell,
Yet still my calmer thoughts his choice commend,
I praise the hermit, but regret the friend;
Who now resolves, from vice and London far,
To breathe in distant fields a purer air,
And, fixed on Cambria's solitary shore,
Give to St. David one true Briton more.
For who would leave, unbribed, Hibernia's land,
Or change the rocks of Scotland for the Strand?
There none are swept by sudden fate away,
But all whom hunger spares with age decay:
Here malice, rapine, accident, conspire,
And now a rabble rages, now a fire;
Their ambush here relentless ruffians lay,
And here the fell attorney prowls for prey;
Here falling houses thunder on your head,
And here a female atheist talks you dead.

SAMUEL JOHNSON (1709–1784)

A mighty mass of brick, and smoke, and shipping,
Dirty and dusky, but as wide as eye
Could reach, with here and there a sail just skipping
In sight, then lost amidst the forestry of masts; a wilderness of
steeples peeping
On tiptoe through their sea-coal canopy;
A huge, dun cupola, like a foolscap crown
On a fool's head—and there is London Town.

∾ LORD BYRON (1788–1824) ∾

To live in London was my young wood-dream,
London, where all the books come from, the lode
That draws into its center from all points
The bright steel of the world; where Shakespeare wrote,
And Eastcheap is, with all its memories
Of gossip quickly, Falstaff, and Prince Hal;
Where the very stones that Milton trod,
And Johnson, Garrick, Goldsmith, and the rest;
Where even now our Dickens builds a shrine
That pilgrims through all time will come to see,
London! Whose street names breathe such home to all:
Cheapside, the Strand, Fleet Street, and Ludgate Hill,
Each name a story in itself.
To live in London! London the buskined stage
Of history, the archive of the past,
The heart, the center of the living world!
Wake, dreamer, to your village and your work.

ROBERT LEIGHTON (1834–1911)

It is a goodly sight through the clear air,
From Hapstead's heathy height to see at once
England's capital in fair expanse,
Towers, belfries, lengthened streets, and structures fair.
St. Paul's high dome amidst the vassal bauds
Of neighboring spires, a regal chieftain stands,
And over fields of ridgy roofs appear,
With distance softly tinted, side by side
In kindred grace, like twain sisters dear,
The towers of Westminster, her Abbey's pride:
While far beyond the hills of Surrey shine
Through thin soft haze, and show their wavy line.
Viewed thus, a goodly sight! But when surveyed
Through denser air when moistened winds prevail,
In her grand panoply of smoke arrayed,
While clouds aloft in heavy volumes sail,
She is sublime. She seems a curtained gloom
Connecting heaven and earth, a threatening sign of doom.

ꞋJOANNA BAILLIE (1854–1919)ꞌ

THOMAS CARLYLE IN 1832

A prophet is not without honor except in his own town, or perhaps in his own time, either. Thomas Carlyle was widely acknowledged, along with William Cobbett, John Ruskin, and William Morris, as one of the great Jeremiahs of the Victorian age. Like them, he railed against the bold materialism, the bare rationalism, and the brazen skepticism of his time with an untempered fervor rivaling the seers of yore. And consequently, he was less than esteemed by his peers. But he has proved more relevant than almost all of them—to our time and to all time.

Chided as a contentious crank, pilloried as a bombastic buffoon, reproached as a jingoistic jester, and dismissed as a domineering dolt, Carlyle nonetheless set the standard for philosophical commentary and almost single-handedly changed the shape of historical research for several generations to come. By turns scholarly and theatrical, sober and whimsical, furtive and satirical, he challenged the staid notions of the dispassionate academic literary establishment and championed the popularization of revisionist and partisan chronicling.

He was born on December 4, 1795, in the small market town of Ecclefechan in the Scottish county of Dumfriesshire, not far from the north shore of the Solway Firth—the eldest of nine children. The roots of his family in that Annandale soil were deep and tena-

cious. His father was a stonemason and a farmer who raised his
progeny in the proud, but stern, providence of the Burgher
Secession Church, one of the numerous splinter groups that had
rebelled against the laxity of the established national church.
Though young Carlyle fled to the intellectual environs of literary
London at the earliest opportunity, he was never to escape the tug of
those strong childhood influences: he was a resolute Scot, he was a
hard-working commoner, and he was a convinced Calvinist. Furious
episodes of rebellion from these standards would punctuate his life
and career but he always returned—thus demonstrating his con-
tention that what a man is ultimately determines what he does, not
the other way around.

Carlyle abandoned his first ambition to be a clergyman for a
career as an economist and mathematician, but before long his wide-
ranging intellect felt too constrained even by that. He read vora-
ciously and omnivorously in the Medieval Classics and the Chansons
de Chivalry realizing before long that his emerging worldview—
rooted in that profound heritage of near-forgotten Christendom—
was utterly at odds with the prevailing Enlightenment view of his
time. So he began to write—or rather to prophesy.

He made his reputation as an enthusiastic translator and an icono-
clastic reviewer—specializing in the prolific new explosion of
German Romanticism. But in 1832 on a visit to the sprawling modern metropolis of London, he began writing his brilliant commen-

tary *Sartor Resartus*. It was his reaction to the compelling attractions and grotesque contradictions of the city.

At the time, London was in the process of becoming the first truly great industrial center in the world. The venerable old city of Shakespeare and Milton and Pope and Dryden and Johnson and Wren was rapidly disappearing. In its place was emerging the remarkable innovative modern machinery of the urban center—the inhuman humanism of commercial progress.

Carlyle was attracted and repulsed simultaneously. And his writing ably demonstrated that wrenching paradox, as did the similarly conflicted novels of his friend Charles Dickens.

Part novel, part autobiography, part history, and part social commentary, *Sartor Resartus* was one of the most original works of prose ever written in the English language. The conservative publishers along Charing Cross Road and Paternoster Row in London were frightened away at first by its ostentatiously fantastic vision and so it was serialized in the newly established *Fraser's Magazine.* Only later—because of intense public demand—was it published independently for the trade.

At first sight, the book appeared to be the bizarre account—recorded by an admiring but dubious editor—of a work by an outlandish German philosopher named Diogenes Teufelsdrockh, (literally: Devil's Dung), who was Professor of Things in General at the University of Weissnichtwo (literally: Don't Know Where) on the

Philosophy of Clothes (or more specifically, on the philosophy of hidden and revealed covenants). The whole story turns out to be an ingenious and amusing metaphor comparing and contrasting Lutheran Pietism with Calvinistic Covenantalism. The eccentricity of Teufelsdrockh is somehow symbolic of God's providential working in the lives of mundane and ordinary men to cause them to accomplish marvelous and extraordinary deeds while his strange fixation on clothes is symbolic of this poor fallen world which at once disguises and conceals, but also reveals and expresses the gracious workings of the Spirit of God behind the spirit of men.

Most students of the work of Carlyle contend that his thought did not reach full maturity until the appearance of his great historical and biographical works—*The French Revolution* in 1837, *Heroes and Hero Worship* in 1841, *Life and Letters of Cromwell* in 1845, *Life of Sterling* in 1851, the multi-volume *History of Frederick the Great* from 1858–1865, and *The Portraits of John Knox* in 1875. But the fact is, the philosophical grid for those later works was first established and best delineated in *Sartor Resartus*.

It was also in the novel that he argues that history is itself a kind of dim Gospel—the veiled revelation of a just providence working in the affairs of men. It was not a Gospel that could be read simplistically, of course, rather it was one that bids us all to, "pause over the mysterious vestiges of Him, whose path is in the great deep of Time, whom history indeed reveals, but only in all of history, and in

Eternity—not merely in swatches—will He clearly be revealed."

Sartor Restartus was also where Carlyle best enunciated his belief that we can see the ultimate reality of God's glory in the brute obscurity of recorded events knowing that, "Man's history is a perpetual Evangel—an inarticulate Bible—a loud-roaring loom of time, with all its French Revolutions and Jewish Revelations weaving the vesture thou seest Him by."

Thus, in the novel he provided his readers with the best—and arguably the most entertaining—introduction to his ground-breaking thought. Thus while reading his works of history—especially of the Revolution and of Frederick—is essential, reading his creatively playful philosophy of history is even more so. And it is necessary if only to enable us to wrestle as he did with the incongruities of life in the throes of urban and industrial modernity.

Eventually, Carlyle moved into the city of paradox and contradiction—and London served as his home and his stimulus for the rest of his life. But it was as a visitor that its compelling power—as both his inspiration and his nemesis—first revealed itself to him and to all the world through his brilliant writing.

An English Dinner Banquet

It may be granted that the English have failed to adequately master the fine culinary arts, nevertheless, they seem entirely unhampered at table. They may not know how to cook but they certainly know how to eat.

Thomas Carlyle (1795–1881)

Hors D'oeuvres: Anchovy Eggs

4 hard-boiled eggs, 4 anchovies, 1 t essence of anchovy, 2 T white sauce, watercress, oil and vinegar, cayenne

Cut the eggs across in halves, remove the yolks carefully, and cut off the extreme end of each half to enable them to stand firmly. Wash, bone, and dry the anchovies, chop them coarsely, and pound them with the yolks until smooth. Add the anchovy essence and the white sauce gradually until a moist paste is formed; then season to taste, and rub through a hair sieve. Fill the egg cases with the preparation, garnish with watercress seasoned with oil and vinegar and cayenne, and serve.

Oysters with Caviar

6 oysters, 6 t seasoned Russian or hygienic caviar, slices of lemon, parsley

Open the oysters and remove the beards. Put 1 t of caviar in each of the lower (deep) shells, and place the oyster on top. Garnish the dish with slices of lemon and sprigs of parsley. Keep on ice until required for table.

Soup Course: Clear Soup of Consommé

2 quarts brown stock, 1 lb. neck of beef (lean, finely chopped or passed two or three times through a sieve), 1 carrot (cut in two or three pieces), 1 onion (left whole), strip of celery, 12 peppercorns, 6 allspice, 2 cloves, salt, whites and shells of 4 eggs

The stock should be cold and quite free from fat. Put it into a clean well-tinned stewpan, add the beef, vegetables, flavourings, seasonings, the shells of the eggs crushed and the whites slightly whisked, and whisk all together over a gentle fire until just on boiling point, then let it simmer about 30 minutes. Strain through a clean dry cloth, reheat, and season to taste before serving. A glass of sherry, a dessert spoonful of French vinegar or lemon juice, and a pinch of castor sugar are frequently added when re-heating the consommé.

Fish Course: Baked Salmon with Caper Sauce

2 slices salmon, about 2 oz. butter, ¹/₂ t chopped parsley, 1 shallot, salt and pepper, grated nutmeg, Caper Sauce

Lay the salmon in a baking dish, place the pieces of butter over it, and add the other ingredients, rubbing a little of the seasoning into the fish. Bake in a hot oven (425°) for about 20 to 35 minutes. Baste frequently, and when done place the salmon on a dish, pour Caper Sauce over it, and serve.

Caper Sauce

½ pint melted butter, 1 T capers either cut in two or coarsely chopped, 1 dessert spoonful of vinegar from the capers, salt and pepper

Melt the butter, add to it the capers, vinegar, and seasoning, and pour over salmon.

Entrée Course: Ragoût of Lamb with Sorrel

2 or 3 lb. neck or breast of lamb, ½ pint boiling stock, 2 ozs. butter, 1 oz. flour, 1 onion, 1 small carrot, 1 strip celery, a bouquet-garni (parsley, thyme, bay-leaf), the yolk of 1 egg, 1 T cream, ¼ pint sorrel purée (or, if more convenient, ¼ pint spinach purée mixed with the juice of half a lemon), salt and pepper

Trim the meat, and blanch it by putting it into cold water, bringing it slowly to a boil, and then immersing it for a few minutes in sea-soned salt water. Drain, dry well, and cut into 2-inch squares. Heat the butter in a stewpan, and fry the sliced vegetables for 15 minutes, but do not let them brown. Now sprinkle in the flour, stir and cook for 3 or 4 minutes, then add the boiling stock, herbs, ¼ t salt, half the quantity of pepper, and stir until smooth. Lay the pieces of meat in the sauce, put on the lid, which should fit closely, and simmer very gently for about 1½ hours. Meanwhile cook the sorrel or spinach, rub it through a fine sieve, and season to taste. When the meat is ready, pile it in the center of a hot dish. Strain the sauce into another stew-pan, and add the sorrel purée; when nearly boiling put in the yolk of egg and cream, previously mixed together, and stir until the sauce thickens. Season to taste, pour over the meat, and serve.

Asparagus Pudding

¼ pint asparagus points, 2 eggs, 2 T flour, 1 T very finely minced ham, 1 oz. butter, pepper and salt to taste, milk

Cut up the nice green tender parts of the asparagus about the size of peas, put them into a basin with the eggs, which should be well beaten, and the flour, ham, butter, pepper, and salt. Mix well and moisten with sufficient milk to make a pudding the consistency of a thick batter. Put it into a buttered pint mould, tie it down with a floured cloth, place it in boiling water, and let it boil for 2 hours. Turn it out of the mould on to a hot dish, and pour plain melted butter round, but not over the pudding.

Roasted Larks

1 dozen larks, butter, 12 slices bacon, 1 egg, breadcrumbs, salt and pepper, croûtes of toasted bread, breadcrumbs, lemon slices, watercress, oil, salt and pepper

Pick and singe the birds, cut off the feet, and remove the gizzards. Truss them in shape by means of a skewer, which should be long enough to hold six. Brush them over with hot butter or fat, cover each breast with a piece of bacon, and roast the birds in a 450° oven for about 10 minutes, basting them constantly. Place each bird on a piece of toast, arrange them in a close circle on a hot dish, fill the centre with hot breadcrumbs, and garnish with cut lemons and watercress seasoned with salad oil, salt, and pepper.

Irish Boiled Potatoes

2 lbs. potatoes, water

Wash and scrub the potatoes, but do not peel them. Put them into a saucepan of boiling water, boil slowly until they can be easily pierced with a fork, then immediately add sufficient cold water to reduce the temperature several degrees below the boiling point. Let them remain for 2 or 3 minutes, then pour off the water, cover the potatoes with a folded cloth, and allow them to stand by the side of the fire until the steam has evaporated. Peel them quickly, and send them to table in an open dish, in order that the steam may escape, otherwise the potatoes may be watery.

Vegetable Marrow, Fried

1 or 2 medium-sized vegetable marrows, egg and breadcrumbs, frying fat, salt, and pepper

Peel and boil the marrows in salt and water until tender, then drain well. Cut them into quarters and remove the seeds. Coat each piece with egg and breadcrumbs, and fry in hot fat until nicely browned. Drain, sprinkle with salt and pepper, and serve.

Salad Course: Celery and Truffle Salad

1 large or 2 small heads of celery, 1 lemon, 3 or 4 large truffles, 1 T Madeira wine, Mayonnaise Sauce

Trim the white part of 1 or 2 heads of celery with its root, and wash thoroughly. Cut it into very fine shreds, and put these into cold water with the juice of 1 lemon to soak. Slice and cut into shreds 3 or 4 large truffles. Drain the celery, and mix with the truffles. To this add 1 tablespoon of Madeira wine (if used), and dress neatly on a glass dish or in a salad bowl. Coat with Mayonnaise Sauce, decorate to taste, and serve.

Mayonnaise Sauce

2 egg yolks, 1 t French mustard, ½ t salt, pinch pepper, 1 pint salad oil, 1 T tarragon vinegar, 1 T cream.

Put the yolks into a basin, add the mustard, salt and pepper, and stir quickly with a wooden spoon. Add the oil, first drop by drop and afterwards more quickly, and at intervals a few drops of the vinegar. By stirring well, the mixture should become the consistency of very thick cream. Lastly, add the cream, stirring all the while. A little cold water may be added if the sauce is found to be too thick.

Sweets Course: St. Cloud Pudding

2 oz. almonds, stale sponge cake, 2 oz. castor sugar, 1 pint strong clear coffee, 3 eggs, ½ gill cream, 3 T apricot marmalade or jam, glacé cherries, angelica

Blanch, shred, and bake the almonds until pale brown. Coat a plain charlotte mould thickly with clarified butter, and sprinkle liberally with the prepared almonds when cold. Fill the mould ¾ full with pieces of cake, interspersing the remainder of the almonds. Dissolve the sugar in the coffee, pour over the well-beaten eggs, stirring meanwhile, and add the cream. Strain into the mould, cover with a buttered paper, and steam very gently for about 2 hours. Turn out and set aside till cold. Dilute the apricot marmalade with a little water, sweeten to taste, and when cool strain over the pudding. Decorate with rings of cherries and strips of angelica.

Savoury Course: Bloater Toast

2 bloaters with soft roes, 1½ oz. butter, 1 egg, salt, cayenne, 8 squares buttered toast

Remove the roes, grill the bloaters, free them from skin and bone, then chop them, and rub them through a fine sieve. Heat 1 oz. butter in a small stewpan, add the fish, and when hot put in the egg, season to taste, and stir by the side of the fire until the mixture thickens. Meanwhile divide the roes into 8 pieces, and fry them in the remainder of the butter. Spread the fish preparation on the croûtes, lay the roe on top, and serve as hot as possible.

Ending Course: Assorted Cheeses and Fruits

Edinburgh

Edinburgh, the historic capital of proud Scotland and one of the most beautiful cities anywhere with its famous castle, medieval Old Town, and stunning panoramic views, is also surrounded by beautiful coast and countryside. With a wide choice of places to visit—castles, palaces, historic neighborhoods and villages, museums and galleries, including the Royal Museums and the National Galleries, the city has long been a favorite destination of travelers the world over. The long walk down the Royal Mile, punctuated by famous churches, an array of literary associations, a stunning selection of rustic handcraft shops, a bevy of antiquarian bookstores, irresistible pubs and taverns, and a palace on either end, is the backbone of both a remarkable city and a remarkable national legacy that reaches back beyond the heroic days of *William Wallace* and *Robert the Bruce* and forward to the rich epoch of *Robert Burns, Walter Scott, Thomas Chalmers,* and *Robert Louis Stevenson.*

Edina! Scotia's darling seat!
         ROBERT BURNS (1759–1796)

A queer compromise between fairyland and battleground is the very quintessence of Edinburgh.
         DEVON MORTON (1888–1951)

Such dusky grandeur clothed the height,
Where the huge castle holds its state,
And all the steep slope down,
Whose ridgy back heaves to the sky,
Piled deep and massy, close and high,
Mine own romantic town.
         SIR WALTER SCOTT (1771–1832)

In Edinburgh there abides, above all things, a sense of its beauty. Hill, crag, castle, rock, blue stretch of sea, the picturesque ridge of the Old Town, the squares and terraces of the New, the quick life of today sounding among the relics of antiquity, and overshadowed by the august traditions of a Kingdom, makes a visit to the city more impressive than perhaps any other.
         ALEXANDER SMITH (1809–1885)

Edinburgh, even were its population as great as that of London, could never be merely a city. Here there must always be present the idea of the comparative littleness of all human works. Here, the proudest of palaces must be content to catch the shadows of mountains; and the grandest of fortresses to appear like the dwellings of pigmies, perched on the very bulwarks of creation.

JOHN LOCKHART (1794–1854)

There is no land with greater pride than Scotland and no city with a greater sense of place than Edinburgh.

JAMES STUART KILMANY (1866–1939)

Old tales, old customs, and old men's dreams
Obscure this town. Memories abound.
In the mild misted air, and in the sharp air
Toga and kilt and gown walk the pier
And the past sleeps in the stones.

JAMES BRUCE (1730–1794)

The place establishes an interest in people's hearts; they go where they will, they find no city of the same distinction; go where they will, they take a pride in their old Edinburgh.

ROBERT LOUIS STEVENSON (1850–1894)

The Scotch are a nation of gentlemen.

      KING GEORGE IV (1762–1830)

O Caledonia, stern and wild,
Meet nurse for a poetic child,
Land of brown heath and shaggy wood
Land of the mountain and the flood.

      SIR WALTER SCOTT (1771–1832)

The Scots are steadfast. But not their clime.

      OLIVER GOLDSMITH (1728–1774)

The high ridge of the Castle Rock and the surging uplift of Arthur's
Seat, with the city set between, affords the most picturesque site for
a city in all of Europe.

      MARK TWAIN (1835–1910)

Scotland, thy weather's like a modish wife,
Thy winds and rains forever are at strife:
So termagant, a while, her thunder tries,
And, when she can no longer scold, she cries.

      AARON HILL (1701–1766)

The halesome parritch, chief of Scotia's food.
ROBERT BURNS (1759–1796)

Scotland's cauld and grey, you say
But it's no' ill to prove
Oor dourest hills are only
Rainbows at a'e remove.
HUGH MACDIARMID (1892–1956)

Take a brief look about the city of Edinburgh and you'll have all the proof you need that gold is a national game. It is as thoroughly Scottish as haggis, cockie-leekie, scotch whisky, kilts, bagpipes, high cheekbones, stout porter, shortbread, tartans, or gean jam.
ANDREW LANG (1827–1892)

Humff hamff quod the Laird of Bamff.
JAMES FERGUSON (1808–1886)

As Scotland is the knuckle-end of England, so Edinburgh is the knuckle-head of London.
LADY LOUISE HAMILTON (1877–1956)

Should auld acquaintance be forgot,
And never brought to mind?
Should auld acquaintance be forgot
And days o' auld lang syne?

For auld lang syne, my dear,
For auld lang syne,
We'll tak' a cup o' kindness yet,
For auld lang syne?

We twa ha'e run about the braes,
And pu't the gowans fine,
But we've wandered mony a weary foot,
Sin'auld lang syne.

We twa ha'e paidl't i' the burn,
Frae mornin' sun till dine,
But seas between us braid ha'e roared,
Sin auld lang syne.

And here's a hand, my trustie fiere,
And gie's a hand o' thine,
And we'll tak' a right guid willie waught,
For auld lang syne.

And surely ye'll be your pint-stoup,
And surely I'll be mine,
And we'll tak' a cup o' kindness yet,
For auld lang syne.

ROBERT BURNS (1759–1796)

The wailing of the pipers, the clattering of the pubs, and the yam-mering of the peddlers make the sounds of Edinburgh unlike those of any other place on earth.

ॐ TRISTAN GYLBERD (1954–) ॐ

In the late evening twilight we went to the palace of Holyrood House where Queen Mary lived and loved. The chapel close to it is now roofless; grass and ivy grow there; and at the broken altar where Mary was crowned Queen of Scotland. Everything around is broken and mouldering, and the bright sky shines in. I believe I found in that old chapel the beginning of my Scotch Symphony.

ॐ FELIX MENDELSSOHN (1809–1847) ॐ

And though, as you remember, in a fit,
Of wrath and rhyme, when juvenile and curly,
I railed at Scots to show my wrath and wit,
Which must be owned was sensitive and surly,
Yet ëtis in vain such sallies to permit,
They cannot quench young feelings fresh and early:
I scotched, not killed, the Scotchman in my blood,
And love the land of mountains and of flood.

ॐ LORD BYRON (1788–1824) ॐ

Samuel Johnson in 1773

He was the most dominant figure of the eighteenth century literary world. The renown of Samuel Johnson was due in part to his moral essays, poetry, and prayers, in part because of his remarkable *Dictionary of the English Language*, and in part because of his amazing novel *Rasselas*. But in spite of all his carefully composed contributions to the prose of his native land, he may have never attained the stature that places him in the same rank as Shakespeare and Milton were it not for his famous trip to Scotland with his friend and biographer, James Boswell.

Born in Litchfield in 1709, the son of a failed bookseller, Johnson struggled throughout his early life against the ravages of poverty. Though he demonstrated a precocious mind and a prodigious literary talent, he was unable to complete his education at Oxford, and instead began his lifelong labors as a hack freelance writer in London for a series of newspapers, magazines, journals, and book publishers. As a result, he became phenomenally prolific and adept at virtually every genre—from criticism, translation, poetry, and biography to sermons, parliamentary reports, political polemics, and dramatic stage plays. Though his work was recognized as brilliant, he was never quite able to climb out of the miry privation that seemed to bog him down throughout his life.

At last, when he was nearly fifty, he received a commission to produce a dictionary. Over the course of the next seven years, he single-handedly took on the great task of comprehensively documenting English usage. The work, when completed, set the standard for etymology forever afterward. It was indeed stunning. Each word was not only carefully and succinctly defined, but illustrated from classic or poetic literature.

The dictionary earned Dr. Johnson a royal allowance which enabled him to pay off his bill collectors and to live with a modicum of ease. It was during this season of his life that he first met James Boswell, a Scottish ne'er-do-well and spendthrift who had already spent half a lifetime squandering his father's considerable estate on the pleasures of the flesh. Johnson was a pious, thoughtful, bookish, and venerable elder statesman. Boswell was an impetuous, ingratiating, bombastic, and irreverent young turk. But amazingly, the two men struck up a fast friendship. Over the next several years, the unlikely pair carried on a conversation that, when documented in Boswell's biographies and journals, would enchant the world.

Boswell had long desired to show off his homeland—and given Dr. Johnson's interest in the lost cause of the Jacobites, of Bonnie Prince Charlie, and of the tragedy of Culloden, the invitation to come to Scotland was entertained with great interest and gratitude. Nevertheless, it was not until 1773 that Johnson actually accepted.

By that time, he was nearly incapacitated with gout, corpulence, and arthritis. By all accounts he was built for the stationary lifestyle rather than the mobile anyway—overweight and slovenly, asthmatic and awkward. First impressions of him always surprised people. He was big-boned, six feet tall, stout, and stooped. Over a crop of wiry, frizzy hair he wore varying, ill-fitting wigs in unfetching shades of gray. His near-sightedness led to his reading so close to lamps and candles that the wigs frequently bore scorch marks. Despite the fact that he was eloquent of speech and elegant of mind, he was hardly a fit candidate for the difficult task of journeying overland any distance. Nevertheless, he set out by coach at the beginning of the month of August to see the city of the Scots.

The city had hardly changed since the Reformation had burst onto the national stage in the middle of the sixteenth century. It still consisted of a small cluster of streets radiating off of the Royal Mile, which stretched from the Castle Rock down to the royal palace of Holyrood. The swampy fens to the north of the city had not yet been filled to create the Princes Street Gardens, Waverly Station, or the Royal Academy grounds. Nor had the great plan for the New Town been laid out. Though a few fashionable neighborhoods and settlements had begun to wrap around Carlton Hill where eventually the Royal Observatory would be built, the city was essentially contained within the narrow confines of the old medieval ridge.

Boswell had arranged for Dr. Johnson to be feted and entertained throughout his stay in the city—and the narrative of his visit is essentially a chronology of conversations, parties, and social occasions. There was much eating, drinking, discussing, debating, haranguing, criticizing, joshing, and kidding over the course of the several days they spent together in the city.

It is evident that what occupied Dr. Johnson more than all the conversations, the meals, and the parties—as much as he apparently enjoyed them—was the history of the land. And Edinburgh was a city steeped in history.

He believed that the principal aim of history was to preserve the practical lessons and profound legacies of Christendom without the petty prejudice of literary or academic fashions and without the parsimonious preference of enlightenment innovations. He wanted to avoid the trap of noticing everything that went unnoticed in the past while failing to notice all that the past deemed notable. He shunned the kind of modern epic that is shaped primarily by the banalities of sterile bureaucratic decrees or the fancies of empty theater scenes rather than the realities of historical facts.

At the same time, though, he believed that history was a series of lively adventure stories—and thus should be told without the cumbersome intrusion of arcane rhetoric or truck-loads of extraneous annotations, caveats, and imprimaturs. In fact, he believed that history was a romantic moral drama in a world steadily enraptured impersonally scientific—and thus should be told with passion, unction, and verve. To him, the record of the ages was actually philosophy teaching by example—and because however social conditions may change, the great underlying qualities which make and save men and nations do not alter, it was the most important example of all. He understood only too well that the past is ever present, giving shape and focus to all our lives—yet it is not what was, but whatever seems to have been, simply because the past, like the future, is part and parcel of the faith. It is no surprise, then, that he sought to comprehend events through the same worldview lens as those who wrought the events in the first place.

In Edinburgh, he reveled in stories of William Wallace and Robert the Bruce. He gloried in the tales of Flora MacDonald and Rob Roy. He marveled at the tenacity of the Covenanters and the duplicity of the Campbells. He listened to the tales of the Grants of Strathspey, of the Stuarts of Stirling, of the Walkers of Loch Ness, of the MacDonalds of Glencoe, and of the Frasers of Iona. He retraced the steps of John Knox along High Street from Gileskirk to Holyrood and he stood transfixed in the Greyfriars churchyard where the signing of the Solemn League and Covenant had toppled a king and forged a nation.

He believed that modern social and political agendas—which are more often than not ferociously alien to the founding principles of Western Christendom—generally demanded a radical and revisionist perspective of history. They manipulated the past in an effort to similarly manipulate the future. So, as an antidote to that kind of dastardly divined despotism, he advocated a very straightforward, back-to-basics, and shirt-sleeves approach to academic and cultural integrity: strip away the layers of historical waffling and garbling that had begun to veil—or even bury—the truth. Indeed, he believed that nearly all the historical work worth doing at that time in the English language was the work of shoveling off heaps of rubbish inherited from the immediate past.

Thus, his trip to Edinburgh proved to be a kind of sociological and cultural version of an archeological expedition. And when his observations, witticisms, epigrams, quips, and aphorisms were ultimately recorded in Boswell's journal and biography, his vision of history not only helped to awaken a new Scottish nationalism among the next generation of Scottish writers, such as Robert Burns and Walter Scott, but also provoked a new approach to the academic discipline of Moral Philosophy as practiced by a new generation of Scottish thinkers, such as Thomas Chalmers and Adam Smith.

Familiarity breeds contempt—though familiar things are all the more remarkable for their comfortable accessibility. So many of the memorable expressions in Shakespeare's *Hamlet* have become proverbial, that once after attending a performance of the play Mark Twain was able to satirically complain that, "It was nothing more than a bunch of cliches." In the same way, certain aspects of Edinburgh's story had become so familiar to many Scots that they were apt to miss their original impact and import. Thus, Dr.

Johnson's inquiries aimed at the familiar as much as the unfamiliar—
in the hope of exchanging contempt for cognizance.

In that, he was successful.

Indulging the passions of the good doctor in his declining years
was therefore more than a matter of social kindness. It was a significant contribution to the shaping of the destiny of the land in accord
with God's good providence.

And that was no mean feat.

A SCOTTISH BREAKFAST

In the breakfast, the Scots, whether of the Lowlands or mountains must be confessed to excel us. The tea and coffee are accompanied not only with butter, but with honey, conserves, and marmalades. If an epicure could remove by a wish in quest of sensual gratification, wherever he had supped, he would breakfast in Scotland.

SAMUEL JOHNSON (1709–1784)

Scots Orange-Chip Marmalade

loaf sugar, Seville oranges, 2 lemons, water, 1 egg white (to clarify sugar)

Take equal weight of fine loaf sugar and Seville oranges. Wipe and grate the oranges, but not too much. (The outer grate boiled up with sugar will make an excellent conserve for rice, custard, or batter puddings.) Cut the oranges the cross way and squeeze out the juice through a small sieve. Scrape off the pulp from the inner skins and remove the seeds. Boil the skins till perfectly tender, changing the water to take off part of the bitter. When cool scrape the coarse, white, thready part from the skins, and, trussing 3 or 4 skins together for dispatch, cut them into narrow chips. Clarify the sugar*, and put the chips, pulp, and juice into it. Add, when boiled for 10 minutes, the juice and grate of 2 lemons to every dozen oranges. Skim and boil for twenty minutes; pot and cover when cold.

*To clarify sugar: To every pound of broken sugar of the best quality take a quarter-pint of water, and the half of the white of an egg beat up, or less egg will do. Stir this up till the sugar dissolves, and when it boils, and the scum rises strong edging the pan forward from the stove till all the scum is thrown up. Set it on the hearth and when it has settled take off the scum with a sugar-skimmer, and lay this on a reversed hair-sieve over a dish, that what syrup is in it may run clear from it. Return the drained syrup into the pan, and boil and skim the whole once more.

Gean Jam

geans (wild cherries), water, sugar, gooseberry or currant juice

Weigh your wild cherries, stone them, and put them into a preserving pan. Cover them with water and boil until nearly all the juice is dried up, about three quarters of an hour. Add sugar, allowing a pound to every 6 pounds of fruit, and gooseberry or currant juice, allowing a pint to every 6 pounds. Boil all together until it jellies (20 to 30 minutes), skimming it well and keeping it well stirred. Pour into pots.

Honey Cakes

½ lb. finely pounded loaf sugar, ¾ lb. honey, 1½ lb. dried and sifted flour, ¼ lb. citron, ½ oz. orange peel cut fine, ¾ oz. pounded ginger and cinnamon

In a pan melt the sugar with the honey and mix in the other ingredients. Roll out the paste and cut it into small cakes of any form. Bake at 350° until lightly brown.

Hot Cross Buns

6 oz. salt butter, 2 lb. flour, 3 eggs, yeast, water, ½ lb. sugar, ½ oz. cinnamon, ½ oz. ginger, nutmeg, cloves

Rub salt butter into flour and break 3 eggs among it in a basin. Add a breakfast-cupful of yeast and mix all together with sufficient tepid water to make it into a thin batter. Cover it up and let it stand all night in a warm place. Mix it up next morning with sugar, cinnamon, ginger, a little grated nutmeg, and a pinch of ground cloves. Mix all well together with as much flour as will keep the dough from sticking to the hands. Allow 2 ounces of dough to each bun and shape them into rounds. Prove them for 1 hour in a steam press or another warm place. Cut some scraps of pastry into thin narrow strips and place these on the buns in the form of a cross. Bake in a quick oven (400°) for a few minutes and glaze with sugar and water.

Paris

*N*owhere does the novelist's prose slip more readily into the normally bland tones of the travel guidebook. Paris is a marvel of vintage sensory delights. The staccato sounds of the clicking of saucers in the Place de la Contrescarpe, the trumpeting of traffic around the Arc de Triomphe, and the conspiratorial whispering on benches in the Jardin de Luxembourg seem to play a jangling Debussy score in the twilight hours. The nostalgic smells of luxuriant perfumes, wine, and brandy; the invigorating odors of croissants, espresso, and cut lavender; and the acrid fumes of tobacco, roasted chestnuts, and salon sautés seem to texture a sweet and subtle Monet upon the canvas of l'entente de la vie. The dominating sights of the yellow towers of Notre Dame, the arched bridges cutting across the satin sheen of the river, and the stately elegance of the Bourbon palaces and pavilions scattered about the city like caches of mercy seem to sculpt a muscular Rodin bronze on the tabla rasa landscape. Paris is renowned as the most romantic city in the world—and for good reason. Visitors have reveled in its sensuous beauty and atmosphere for centuries.

No one can spend any length of time in Paris without being captivated by satyrs or muses or cupids or baccuses or all of them together.

  VICTOR HUGO (1802–1885)

Once our boys have seen gaiety of Paris, how will we ever get them to return again to the farms of Iowa and Indiana?

  GENERAL JOHN J. PERSHING (1860–1948)

Why would anyone even wish to return to the farm once they had visited the greatest city in the world—and why would anyone wish it for them?

  MARSHAL FERDINAND FOCH (1851–1929)

Everything about Paris assumes an importance that seems all out of proportion to its actual place in the world. It is all a little larger than life, all a bit exaggerated. Why, even the Hundred Years War between its loyal patriots and London's partisans was somehow extended beyond the bounds of a mere century—dragging on from 1337 to 1453.

  JAMES STUART KILMANY (1866–1939)

Paris strains at her moorings, the river eddies round the stone prow where tall poplars stand like masts, and mist rises about the decaying houses which seventeenth century nobles raised on their meadows. Yielding asphalt, sliding waters, long windows with iron bars set in damp walls, anguish and fear: this is Paris. Rendez-vous des Mariniers, Hotel de Lauzun: this is the moment of the night when the saint's blood liquefies, when the leaves shiver and presentiments of loss stir within the dark coil of our fatality.

CYRIL CONNOLLY (1903–1974)

I am delighted, enchanted, amused, and interested and think I never saw anything more beautiful and gay than Paris.

QUEEN VICTORIA (1819–1901)

Paris is the city of love and folly.

JOHN MILTON (1608–1674)

Such is the intoxicating gaiety of French manners, such the fascination of French amusement, so easy is admission to their public places, libraries, collections, that, though most men enter Paris with disgust, no man ever left it with disappointment.

M. H. HAYDON (1737–1806)

There was a time when to speak ill of Paris was to brand oneself as a barbarian. Times have changed. Today, from Glenda Slaggs and the Lunchtime O'Boozes to the highest reaches of the intelligentsia the cry goes up that Paris is both a clip joint and a cultural desert, an architectural eyesore and a gastronomic poor relation to Soho. Paris, a prominent British intellectual told me, is in danger of pricing itself out of civilization. From all these views, I beg to differ. For me Paris is easily the most agreeable capital in the world to live in. I would define it simply as a city where a civilized man can still lead a civilized life against a civilized background and consider it not a feat of escapism but as something amounting to total immersion. It still remains a city manageable in size, easy to get about in and easy to get out of, with each area retaining an individual character. And it still remains lived in for the greater part by the people who actually work in it. This of course makes an enormous difference to life as compared to most other modern cities which each day gorge and disgorge millions of commuters leaving only a desolation of sterile office blocks behind them. Nothing like this, needless to say happens in Paris and this is particularly noticeable at weekends when most modern cities become graveyards while Paris becomes a playground.

❦ SAMUEL WHITE (1901–1979) ❧

It was a pleasure to eat where everything was so tidy, the food so well cooked, the waiters so polite, and the coming and departing company so moustached, so fisky, so affable, so fearfully and wonderfully Frenchy. They were tidy, noiseless, glided hither and thither, hovered like butterflies, quick to comprehend, and thankful for a gratuity. That is the strangest curiosity yet—a really polite hotel waiter who isn't an idiot.

MARK TWAIN (1835–1910)

In the first place, the town is so beautiful and the people so genteel that it is a real amusement to simply drive about the streets.

LADY SARAH LENNOX (1742–1788)

The French are always open, familiar, and talkative. In Paris, everyone aims at gaiety and sprightliness of behavior and thinks it an accomplishment to be brisk and lively.

JOSEPH ADDISON (1672–1719)

I was taken for a Frenchman. I am insolent. I talk a great deal. I am loud and peremptory. I sing and dance and go along. And lastly, I spend a monstrous deal of money in powder.

LORD CHESTERFIELD (1694–1773)

Other nations are at peace with France; but France is never at peace. The psychology of the Parisian is the psychology of war.

ᴏʄ G. K. CHESTERTON (1874–1936) ʄᴏ

One may walk about Paris and see stones and windows that are still alive with the long business of the city. There is the room where Madame de Sévigné wrote, there is the long gallery where Sully paced, recognizing the new power of artillery and planning the greatness of his master. You may stand on the very floor where the priests stood when St. Louis held the Crown of Thorns above them, more than six hundred years ago; you may stand on the stone that covers Geoffrey Plantagenet before the altar of the cathedral; you may touch the altar the boatmen raised under Tiberius to their gods when our Lord was preaching in Galilee, and as you marvel at that stone you may note around you the little Roman bricks that stood in the same arches when Julian saw them, sitting at the Council that saved the Faith for the West. All these old things remain in this moving, and yet unchanging town.

ᴏʄ HILAIRE BELLOC (1870–1953) ʄᴏ

One might just as effectually argue with a horse as with a Parisian postilion.

of LADY ELIZABETH CRAVEN (1739–1787) ‡o

How they hate us, these foreigners in Paris. What lies they tell of us: how gladly they would see us humiliated. They hate us because we are stupid, hard to please, and intolerably insolent and air-giving.

of WILLIAM THACKERAY (1811–1863) ‡o

We will not let thee be, for thou art ours.
We thank thee still, though thou forget these things,
For that hour's sake when thou didst wake all powers
With a great cry that God was sick of kings.

Leave thee there groveling at their rusted greaves,
These hulking cowards on a painted stage,
Who, with imperial pomp and laurel leaves,
Show their Marengo—one man in a cage.

These, for whom stands no type or title given
In all the squalid tales of gore and pelf;
Though cowed by crashing thunders from all heaven,
Cain never said, my brother slew himself.

Tear you the truth out of your drivelling spy,
The maniac who you set to swing death's scythe.
Nay; torture not the torturer—let him lie:
What need of racks to teach a worm to writhe?

Bear with us, O our sister, not in pride,
Nor any scorn we see thee spoiled of knaves,
But only shame to hear, where Danton died,
Thy foul dead kings all laughing in their graves.

Thou has a right to rule thyself; to be
The thing thou wilt; to grin, to fawn, to creep;
To crown these clumsy airs; ay, and we
Who knew thee once, we have a right to weep.

     G. K. CHESTERTON (1874–1936)

In France all is clockwork, all is order. They make no mistakes. Every third man wears a uniform and whether he be a Marshall of the Empire or a brakeman on a train, he is ready and perfectly willing to answer all your questions with tireless politeness, ready to tell you which car to take, yea and ready to go and put you into it to make sure that you shall not go astray. No, they have no railroad accidents to speak of in France. But why? Because when one occurs somebody has to hang for it. Not hang maybe, but be punished at least with such vigor of emphasis as to make negligence a thing to be shuddered at.

ᴥ MARK TWAIN (1835–1910) ᴥ

We are always assured that Paris is at her loveliest when the chestnuts are in flower and the weeping willows planted below the quays stretch their tendrils towards the passing Seine. The month of May does certainly emphasize and embellish the panoramic aspect of the great city, but not its intimacy. I prefer the early winter evenings when the sky is red behind what was once the Trocadero and the windows of the cafés glimmer through a haze of steam. For me the smell of chestnuts roasting evokes more pleasant memories than any aroused by the candelabra of spring.

ᴥ HAROLD NICOLSON (1886–1968) ᴥ

CHARLES DICKENS IN 1863

The fountains fell with a wintry delicacy into a framing space in the Place de la Concorde. Blue hues crept out from behind the Colonades in the Rue de Rivoli and through the grillwork of the Tuileries. The low, elegant outlines of the Louvre were a serious metallic gray against the setting sun. Well-tended branches hung brooding over animated cafés, embracing conversations with tender intimacy. Long windows opened onto iron-clad balconies in marvelously archaic hotels, while gauzy lace curtains fluttered across imagined hopes and wishes and dreams. Romance wafted freely in the sweet, cold breezes off the Seine.

Charles Dickens found the allure of Paris at Christmas completely irresistible. It was, after all, the most exotic city in the world. It seemed to stimulate in him a serene, secure sense of hope. And hope was something he desperately needed at that stage in his life. He was by all accounts, a tormented man—unhappy in his domestic life, dissatisfied with his public life, and suffering from a myriad of illnesses. As he had so many times before, he had come to Paris for solace, inspiration, and reflection.

He had burst onto the literary scene in his native England some thirty years before with a series of prose sketches published in a monthly magazine and later in a daily newspaper. The twenty-four-year-old author was suddenly thrust to the forefront of celebrity and fame. The stunning success of those first sketches—later published in book form as *Sketches by Boz* and *The Pickwick Papers*—was followed in quick succession by *Oliver Twist, Nicholas Nickleby, David Copperfield, Bleak House, Hard Times, A Tale of Two Cities,* and *Great Expectations.* There was little doubt that Dickens had become the most influential novelist in the English language. His plots, his characters, and his images defined for many the Victorian dystopic standard. But more than that, his prolificacy, his versatility, and his creativity defined the modern literary standard. As G. K. Chesterton later said, "The boors in his books are brighter that the wits in other books."

Born in 1812, the second of eight children, his earliest memories were supremely unhappy. His father, who was a lowly government clerk, was imprisoned for his debts and the young Dickens was sent off to labor in the dismal factories and workhouses of the day. His education was necessarily postponed until he was a teenager—he thus had the odd experience of going from the world to school instead of from school to the world.

The shame of that difficult and impoverished childhood apparently haunted Dickens for the rest of his life—shaping his literary and political sensibilities. When he was finally able to escape his pauper's beginnings, he devoted his abundant gifts to shining a searchlight of scrutiny on the lives of the poor, the frustrated, and the unfulfilled. He memorialized his sense of terrified smallness by holding his boy-

hood horrors to his breast. That sense of tragedy would be his hallmark until his dying day. But he capitalized on his grief—and in the
process, he achieved the great paradox of at once making poetry and
making money.

He became the Victorian equivalent of a rock star—rich, famous,
pampered, and lionized. His was a rags-to-riches dream come true.
Never entirely comfortable with his exalted role though, Dickens
began a deep and impassioned search for a role with which he could
feel at ease. He tried his hand at lecturing. He dabbled in acting and
theater production. He launched innumerable journals, tabloids,
magazines, and newspapers. Finding little satisfaction even in these
professional successes, he turned to arcane philosophies and sundry
esoterica. He explored the occult. And he sated himself in the pleasures of the flesh.

But the great fascination of his life was the Christian faith. At the
heart of most of his novels is evidence of an impassioned quest for
significance—in and through the spiritual system that ultimately
gave flower to the wonder of Western civilization. He wrote countless essays on the disparity between Christian teaching and Christian
practice. He lectured widely on the nature of Christian ethics and
society. And he penned a groping, probing, yearning sketch of the
life of Christ.

But the forum for his most sophisticated musings on the faith
came in his annual Christmas stories. There, he not only rehearsed

his own tragedies and commemorated his own injuries, but he cast about for some metaphysical meaning or comfort for them.

The stories were written beginning in 1843, when Dickens was at the pinnacle of his writing prowess. The first—and probably the best—was *A Christmas Carol*. It is the familiar story of Scrooge, Marley, Cratchit, Tiny Tim, and ghosts from the past, present, and future. It is also the recollection of that strange mixture of joys and sorrows, victories and defeats, sanctities and perversities, approbations and imprecations inherent in this poor fallen world.

With unsurpassed artistry, Dickens painted a picture of depravity, dispossession, and depression with an impressionistic palate—while vividly portraying the power of repentance, redemption, and resurrection with the clarity of a photo. This was undoubtedly the master at his best. Not only did Dickens do something special for Christmas, but Christmas does something special for Dickens.

It was not surprising then to find him in his favorite city at Christmas, seeking fresh vision for the remaining days of his life. He had been able to secure a small attic apartment just blocks away from the university campus in central Paris. It was in a delightful eighteenth century building replete with high ceilings, ornamented plaster bas-relief across one wall, huge shuttered windows, antique furniture, and shelves of dusty old books.

Each day, he would wander over to the Pont Neuf bridge to explore the wares of the bouquinistes—the traditional French booksellers who had pioneered their unique brand of transportable trade early in the seventeenth century. He would then visit one of the many magnificent museums or perhaps eat a picnic lunch in the Bois de Boulogne, the huge park along the city's western ridge. Often, he would end up gawking at the jubilant carnival atmosphere at the Champs de Mars just below the place where the Eiffel Tower would eventually be built for Exposition Universelle in 1889.

Nearly every evening, he left his apartment, crossed over to the Ile de la Cité and approached Notre Dame. He walked beside the great cathedral along the Rue de Cloître. Its magnificence subsumed him in lofty thoughts of rapture and refreshment.

Architecture is a litmus test for the character of a culture. After all, the most valuable things in any human society are those permanent and irrevocable things—things like families. And architecture comes nearer to being permanent and irrevocable than any other man-made craft simply because it is so difficult to dispose of. A book may be torn to pieces, a painting may be hidden in a closet, a symphony may be ignored, but a spire flung toward heaven poses procedural difficulties to all but the most fiercely determined suppressors.

According to the great medieval builder and designer Michel di Giovanni, "Church architecture ought to be an earthly and temporal fulfillment of the Savior's own prophesy that though the voices of men be still, the rocks and stones themselves will cry out with the laud and praise and honor due unto the King of kings and the Lord of lords."

One look at Notre Dame—or virtually any cathedral in Europe, for that matter—and it becomes readily apparent that in spite of all other possible shortcomings, medieval Parisians clearly comprehended that mandate. Taking their cue from the vast treasury of Biblical symbolism, those pioneers of Western culture left us a glorious heritage that continues to this day to translate sight into insight.

Everything in the multifaceted design of the thirteenth century cathedral straddling the Seine—whether consciously or unconsciously—reflected some profound theological conception. Towers, spires, buttresses, bells, porches, gargoyles, aisles, transepts, naves, chancels, vaults, ambulatories, stained glass windows, sacristies, iconostases and narthexes were not simply pragmatic designations on a floor plan. They were integral aspects of the message those early congregants in Paris wished to convey.

But what struck Dickens as he stood there each night was that they were also entirely unnecessary. They were unnecessary because beauty is never necessary. It is never functional or useful, because beauty somehow transcends the categories of the pragmatic. As theologian Alexander Schmemann has said, "When, expecting someone we love, we put a beautiful tablecloth on the table and decorate it with candles and flowers, we do all this not out of necessity, but out of love. As long as Christians love the Kingdom of God, and not only discuss it, they will represent it and signify it in art and beauty and theologically pregnant architecture."

He knew that the Bible taught that the Holy Spirit always establishes a visible glory environment around the Throne of God—sometimes with clouds or flames, sometimes with angels or stars, sometimes with pure light or rainbows, and sometimes with burnished metals or precious stones. Historically, the architectural precedent seen in this remarkable glory environment—whether portrayed in the Garden of Eden, in Noah's Ark, in the desert Tabernacle, in the Temple, or in the New Heavens and New Earth—was taken to be the norm for church architecture. Just as the glory environment proclaims the majesty of the Sovereign Lord, it only made sense to those earlier Christians that the environment of the church should proclaim it as well. They believed their churches should be Biblical, and that they should be simultaneously beautiful—going beyond the necessary. They believed, in other words, that the rocks and stones themselves should cry out: "Hosanna to the King."

Dickens saw all that and more. He wondered what it must have been like to have faith like that—culture-transforming faith. And he wondered if such faith could ever again exist in this poor fallen world. A beautiful civilization can make a person either love beauty or take it utterly for granted. A free civilization can either encourage responsibility or smother it. A great civilization can either spark the flames of faith or snuff them out. A civilization is a terrible and unpredictable thing.

As he returned to his apartment, he habitually walked toward the Pont au Change where the Seine formed a sort of pool traversed by a swift current. It was a place feared by boatmen—a lonely, treacherous place. He invariably leaned over the parapet and gazed into the rushing waters recollecting the sum of his sorrows. It was during such odd sepulchral moments—those moments that immediately precede midnight—that he attempted to reconcile his faltering faith with his halting life.

Did he ever find the peace he was looking for? No one knows. There are hints of an answer in *Our Mutual Friend*, the book he had just begun to write and the last he would complete. One thing is certain, his visit to Paris that winter was both the context for and the climax of that search.

LUNCHEON IN PARIS

There is little in life more settling, more delightful, indeed, more civilized than a luncheon alongside the Seine—perhaps at a little sidewalk café.

CHARLES DICKENS (1812–1870)

Watercress Soup

1½ c watercress, 2 t butter, 6 c stock, salt and pepper, 1 egg yolk, beaten, stale or toasted bread

Chop the watercress and place it in a heavy pot over a low flame until the leaves are wilted and some of the water has evaporated. Add the butter, stock, and season to taste. Cook on low for ten minutes. Add a little soup to beaten egg yolk, then add mixture into soup. Heat thoroughly, but do not boil. Place the bread in a soup bowl. Pour over the toasted bread to serve.

Soufflé aux Frommages (Cheese Soufflé)

¼ c butter, ½ c flour, 1 c milk, ¼ t salt, 4 eggs, separated, ¼ lb. Gruyère cheese, 1/4 lb. Emmental cheese

In a pan melt the butter and stir in the flour. When it is blended, add milk and salt. Stir until mixture thickens. Remove from flame and cool. Beat egg yolks well and add to mixture. Add cheeses. Beat egg whites until stiff and add to the mixture gently. Bake 20 minutes in a medium oven.

Aubergines avec Champignons (Eggplants with Mushrooms)

2 small eggplants, 2 t fat, ¹/₂ lb., chopped parsley, 1 leek, finely chopped, 2 cloves garlic, chopped, ¹/₂ lb. mushrooms, coarsely chopped, red wine

Wash the eggplants and cut them in half. Remove the pulp and chop. Heat the fat in a sauté pan and sauté the parsley, leek, garlic, mushrooms, and eggplant pulp. Fill the eggplants with this mixture and place in a heated dish. Moisten with wine, bake for 30 minutes in a hot oven.

Terrine de Fois de Volailles (Terrine of Chicken Livers)

2 T butter, salt, pepper, chicken livers, pork fat, rosemary, sage, thyme, ¹/₄ c Madeira wine, ¹/₄ c Cognac

Melt 2 tablespoons butter in a sauté pan. Salt and pepper livers and quickly sauté them until just brown on the outside. Cut the pork fat into small pieces, and push the livers and fat through a fine sieve. Add rosemary, sage, and thyme, and ¹/₄ c each of Madeira wine and Cognac. Mix thoroughly. Place in a chicken skin, then in a pan and bake in a medium oven (350°) for 1 hour. Remove the skin, decorate the terrine, and serve in slices.

Compôte de Poires au Vin Rouge
(Pear Compote in Red Wine)

6 pears, ²/₃ c sugar, ³/₄ c water, juice of ¹/₂ lemon, ¹/₄ c sweet red wine

Peel the pears, leaving stems attached. In a saucepan heat the sugar and water. Add the lemon juice. Add the fruit and simmer until it is tender, but not soft. Add the wine just before removing pears from the syrup to serve.

Venice

*T*he city of Venice—with its great plazas crisscrossed by canals which are in turn plied by gondolas—has long had the aura of one of the world's most romantic cities. At one time it was the capital of a sprawling commercial and military empire that stretched all along the Adriatic Sea and across the Mediterranean Sea. Straddling the worlds of both East and West, the city was adorned with rich history, resplendent art, and stunning architecture—all the spoils of a mercantile empire that was the envy of the world. No Grand Tour was complete without a long sojourn in the city. Its riches dazzled even the most jaded, its churches inspired even the most worldly, and its cuisine tantalized even the dullest of sensibilities. It always has been, as one of its ruling Doges brashly asserted, a kind of inescapable geography of poetry, symmetry, and bliss.

Venice is a sort of mystical, magical, fairyland city, settled into the sea, only to arise miraculous upon the florid foundations of verdant medieval stone.

Ↄ T. M. MORRISON (1799–1883) ↄ

All the aspirations of civilization find their well-spring, their genesis, their parturition, their ancestry, their nativity, their derivation, their pedigree, their noel, their yuletide, their lineage, and their birth in Venice.

Ↄ JOHN LASKO (1772–1859) ↄ

In Venice, Tasso's echoes are no more,
And silent rows the songless gondolier;
Her palaces are crumbling to the shore,
And music meets not always now the ear:
Those days are gone, but beauty still is here.
States fall, arts fade, but Nature doth not die,
Nor yet forget how Venice once was dear,
The pleasant place of all festivity,
The revel of the earth, the masque of Italy.

Ↄ LORD BYRON (1788–1924) ↄ

The commonwealth of Venice in their armory have this inscription:
Happy is that city which in time of peace thinks of war.

Ↄ ROBERT BURTON (1577–1640) ↄ

Round the walls of porches there are set pillars of variegated stones, jasper, and porphyry, and deep-green serpentine spotted with flakes of snow, and marbles, that half refuse and half yield to the sunshine, Cleopatra-like, their bluest veins to kiss the shadow, as it steals back from them, revealing line after line of azure undulation, as a receding tide leaves the waved sand; their capitals rich with interwoven tracery, rooted knots of herbage, and drifting leaves of acanthus and vine, and mystical signs, all beginning and ending in the Cross; and above them, in the broad archivolts, a continuous chain of language and of life—of angels, and the signs of heaven, and the labors of men, each in its appointed season upon the earth; and above these, another range of glittering pinnacles, mixed with white arches edged with scarlet flowers—a confusion of delight, amidst which the breasts of the Greek horses are seen blazing in their breadth of golden strength, and the St. Mark's lion, lifted on a blue field covered with stars, until at last, as if in ecstasy, the crests of the arches break into a marble foam, and toss themselves far into the blue sky in flashes and wreaths of sculptured spray, as if the breakers on the Lido shore had been frost-bound before they fell, and the sea-nymphs had inlaid them with coral and amethyst.

JOHN RUSKIN (1819–1900)

I gaze at the palazzo façade in the light. I move toward the light, and my heart shifts its weight when I pass into it, into the clear light—I feel myself in Venice to be at home in the amoral grandiloquence of the light. Here I see the city's centuries old indugence in the profane and its invention of secular grace.

ᴏᵻ HAROLD BRODKEY (1930–1996) ᵻᴏ

What a charm of evening time: to walk up and down the Piazza of Swan Marco as the stars are brightening and look at the grand dim buildings, and the flocks of pigeons flitting about them; or to walk on to the Bridge of La Paglia and look along the dark canal that runs under the Bridge of Sighs—its blackness lit up by a gaslight here and there, and the plash of the oar of blackest gondola slowly advancing.

ᴏᵻ GEORGE ELIOT (1819–1880) ᵻᴏ

Such is the beauty of Venice: the vast tower of St. Mark seems to lift itself visibly from the level field of chequered stones; and, on each side, the countless arches prolong themselves into ranged symmetry, as if the rugged and irregular houses that pressed together above us in the dark alley had been struck back into sudden obedience and lovely order, and all their rude casements and broken walls had been transformed into arches charged with goodly sculpture, and fluted shafts of delicate stone.

ᴏᵻ JOHN RUSKIN (1819–1900) ᵻᴏ

Once Venice was the Autocrat of Commerce; her mart was the great commercial center, the distributing house from whence the enormous trade of the Orient was spread abroad over the Western world. But though that glory has departed, abundant evidence of its splendor remains.

ᴑ MARK TWAIN (1835–1910) ᴑ

I loved her from my boyhood; she to me
Was as a fairy city of the heart,
Rising like water-columns from the sea,
Of joy the sojourn, and of wealth the mart;
And Otway, Radcliffe, Schiller, Shakespeare's art,
Had stamp'd her image in me.

ᴑ LORD BYRON (1788–1824) ᴑ

The gods returned to earth when Venice broke
Like Venus from the dawn encircled sea.
Wide laughed the skies with light when Venice woke
Crowned of antiquity
And like a spoil of gems unmined on earth
Art in her glorious mind
Jeweled all Italy for joy's rebirth
To all mankind.

ᴑ WILLIAM ROSE BENET (1886–1945) ᴑ

In Venice there arises a vision out of the earth, and all the great square of St. Mark seems to have opened from it in a kind of awe, that we may see it far away—a multitude of pillars and white domes, clustered into a long low pyramid of colored light; a treasureheap, it seems, partly of gold, and partly of opal and mother of pearl, hollowed beneath into five great vaulted porches, ceiled with fair mosaic, and beset with sculpture of alabaster, clear as amber and delicate as ivory—sculpture fantastic and involved, of palm leaves and lilies, and grapes and pomegranates, and birds clinging and fluttering among the branches, all twined together into an endless network of buds and plumes; and in the midst of it, the solemn forms of angels, sceptered, and robed to the feet, and leaning to each other across the gates, their figures indistinct among the gleaming of the golden ground through the leaves beside them, interrupted and dim, like the morning light as it faded back among the branches of Eden, when first its gates were angel-guarded long ago.

᚛ JOHN RUSKIN (1819–1900) ᚜

I stood in Venice on the Bridge of Sighs
A palace and a prison on each hand:
I saw from out the wave her structures rise
As from the stroke of the enchanters wand:
A thousand years their cloudy wind expand
Around me, and a dying glory smiles
O'er the far times, when many a subject land
Look'd to the winged Lion's marble piles,
Where Venice sat in state, thron'd on her hundred isles.

LORD BYRON (1788–1824)

This Venice, which was a haughty, invincible, magnificent republic
for nearly fourteen hundred years, whose armies compelled the
world's applause whenever and wherever they battled, whose navies
well-nigh held dominion of the seas and whose merchant fleets
whitened the remotest oceans with their sails and loaded these piers
with the products of every clime, is fallen prey to a poverty, neglect,
and melancholy decay.

MARK TWAIN (1835–1910)

DANTE ALIGHIERI IN 1302

Dante Alighieri was born and raised in the vibrant pre-Renaissance environment of Medieval Florence. His family was descended from minor nobility and he was able to maintain a solidly bourgeois status throughout his life. At various times, he served as a cavalryman in the Florentine army, as an apothecary in the local guild of physicians, as an ambassador in the city's diplomatic corps, as a political administrator for the municipal government, and as an envoy in service to the papacy. But his promising public career came to an end in 1301. He fell out of favor when the political climate in the city changed dramatically and he was eventually banished.

But what was by all appearances a tragic turn of events for Dante, proved to be a propitious and beneficent gift to posterity. It was while he was skulking about Venice in exile that he wrote the bulk of his immortal poetic trilogy, *The Divine Comedy*.

If Venice were not known for her stunning architecture, for her romantic canals, for her feats of commercial prowess, for her naval dominance, for her glorious art, for her sumptuous cuisine, or for her singing gondoliers, she would still have to be remembered for this: Dante was given sanctuary there; and there Dante composed some of the most sublime verses ever set down by mere mortal man.

The masterful work is a kind of spiritual autobiography, mapping the subterranean ecology of his soul. It is an epic allegorical description of a journey through Hell (Inferno), Purgatory (Purgatorio), and finally Heaven (Paradisio). Utilizing soaring images, complex rhyming schemes, brisk plotting, compelling characterizations, and gripping contemporary illustrations, he both created a new vision for vernacular poetry and a new perspective of human psychology. The result is nothing short of stunning.

According to Harold Bloom, besides Shakespeare, "No other literary master, working in any language, so compellingly stretches the boundaries of human creativity, divine passion, and angelic beauty." Arthur Qiller-Couch stated that *Inferno* "broke every literary mold and shattered every artistic expectation." Dante's "eloquence, vitality, and sheer expansive poetic vision," he said "elegantly reshaped the whole scope of epic literature as only a Homer, a Milton, or a Shakespeare ever has." John Buchan asserted that Dante's *Inferno* was "an essential first component of a well-rounded education, the initial course in a curriculum of wisdom and delight. It is at the core of the Western canon."

The brilliance of Dante's vision was almost immediately recognized throughout the Western world. Samuel Johnson claimed that Dante's poetic vision "was the seminal creative impulse which spawned the great literary flowering of High Medievalism and was the enlightening portent of all which would follow in the Renaissance." Indeed, Geoffrey Chaucer, Thomas Malory, Giovanni Boccaccio, and Francesco Petrarch all counted him as a vital primary influence and stirring inspiration for their own pioneering work. He was among the first thinkers and poets to attempt a thoroughgoing integration of Christian ideals with the culture of Pagan antiquity—a conception which would ultimately become a cornerstone of Renaissance thought, life, and culture.

Though brimming over with historical and political ideas, issues, and personalities, *Inferno* is not essentially a covert work of social commentary—an attempt to lampoon political enemies or spiritual-ize ideological agendas. Neither is it an attempt to paint an accurate portrait of an actual Hell or Heaven—though it certainly draws upon traditional Catholic teachings for its prevailing images. It is instead an allegory aimed at an exploration of the human psyche. It is an expansive Humanistic discourse on the nature of virtue and vice, achievement and despair, redemption and damnation, glorifica-tion and vilification. Mingling the Christian wisdom of Augustine, Aquinas, Boethius, and Cassiodorus with the Heathen aesthetic of Virgil, Ovid, Thucidides, and Plutarch, it is a symbolic investigation into the essence of grace and disgrace, orthodoxy and heresy, eternal and temporal, spiritual and carnal.

Dante presages the radical shift in Christendom from the prevail-ing orthodoxy of High Medievalism to the corrosive Humanism of the Renaissance. Indeed, it is pioneered by him. Thus, it might be stated with fairness that he was the first prophet of Modernity. Though neither primarily political nor theological, his work essen-

tially marks the beginning of the end of the Old World Order—
thus, its impact may well have been far more profound than any of
the political tracts or theological tomes of his day.

Dante, believing that he has somehow strayed from the "true
way" into worldly woe, tells of a terrifyingly detailed vision he had—
a vision in which he travels through all the levels of Hell, up the
mount of Purgatory, and finally through the realms of Paradise,
where he is at last allowed a brief glimpse of God.

In the vision, he sets out the night before Good Friday, and finds
himself in the middle of a dense and foreboding forest. There he
encounters three symbolic beasts: a leopard (representing lust), a
lion (representing pride), and a she-wolf (representing covetousness).
Providentially, his chief ideals of womanhood, the Florentine beauty
Beatrice and the Virgin Mary, see his grave predicament and send
the long-dead Roman poet, Virgil, to guide him toward safety.

Virgil and Dante pass through the gates of Hell—inscribed with
the ominous words: "Abandon all hope, all who enter here." With
great trepidation, the two venture onward. They discover that Hell
is a vast funnel-shaped pit, into which is carved some twenty-four
terraces or circles, each a standing place for those individuals judged
guilty of particular sins.

The pilgrims observe—and even speak with—those souls in tor-
ment. To their amazement they encounter hundreds of famous men
and women from both the distant past of antiquity and the more

recent past of Florentine politics—each of whom represents some heinous sin. Dante promises many of those forgotten souls that he will write of their plight if and when he returns to the mortal realm above.

Dante entitled his three-volume work *The Comedy*. The term "comedy" is used in its classical sense to denote a story that begins in great suspense but ends well. Though quite disturbing, the pilgrimage does indeed end well. Dante and Virgil pass through Hell, escape the maws of Satan, climb through Purgatory, venture into outer space, and emerge at the very threshold of Heaven. There, Mary and Beatrice meet them again and set the whole of the journey into its appropriate context.

Clearly, the story is not intended to be taken literally, nor is the symbolism of the nether realm intended to be a mere literary device to shield the author's social and political commentary. It is an allegory. Thus there are two parallel lines of thought that a reader must track. On the one hand an understanding of who the characters are requires some acquaintance with late Medieval politics, Classical literature, and Latin theology. On the other hand a good grasp of the meaning of each encounter requires some awareness of Medieval symbolism, poetic devices, and courtly love. Everything from the profane phrasing of the netherworld conversations and the ethereal descriptions of the loftier realms to the complex symbolic use of numbers and the terza rima rhyming scheme plays a significant role in developing Dante's vision.

By combining so many different devices, symbols, historical references, and contemporary themes—and all utilizing his native Tuscan dialect—Dante created a revolutionary work. It presciently laid the foundations of Renaissance literature and philosophy. It was quickly recognized as a masterpiece. Indeed, it was so highly regarded that shortly after his death, the title was changed from *The Comedy* to *The Divine Comedy*.

How appropriate then that it should have been composed to a large degree in Venice, a divine city that earlier had practically invented the ethos of medieval mystery and then later wrenched the Italian city-states toward the Renaissance with its expansive vision and voracious appetites. Theirs was an unplanned and undesired partnership—but one that ultimately shaped the destiny of men and nations in ways that perhaps neither alone could ever have.

A VENETIAN FÊTE

He gorged as if at a sumptuous Venetian fête.
DANTE ALIGHIERI (1265–1321)

Venetian Bean and Pasta Soup

½ lb. fresh pork rind (cut into small cubes), ¼ lb. salt pork (cut into small cubes), 2 T olive oil, 1 c dried kidney beans, 1 large onion, chopped, ¼ t cinnamon, 1 strip proscuitto, black pepper to taste, 6 c water, 2 c pasta, salt to taste, Parmesan cheese

Sauté the pork rind and salt pork in hot olive oil. Add the beans, onion, cinnamon, proscuitto, pepper, and water. Bring to a boil, lower heat, and simmer for at least 2 hours. Add the pasta and cook for 10 to 12 more minutes. Add salt if necessary and serve in individual bowls, topping with Parmesan cheese.

Squid and Shrimp with Pasta

12 fresh baby squid, 24 shrimp, juice of 1 lemon, ¾ c butter, 1 lb. pasta, 1 c fish stock, salt and pepper to taste

Clean, wash, and trim the squid, discarding inedible parts. Slice crosswise to make thin circles. Peel the shrimp, discarding head and tail. Devein and wash carefully. Sprinkle with lemon juice. In heavy pot, heat ½ c butter. Sauté squid pieces about 10 minutes. To squid, add shrimp and sauté for another 5 minutes. Cook the pasta, drain, and return to pot it was cooked in. Toss the pasta with remaining butter (can substitute olive oil). Add the fish stock, squid, and shrimp, season with salt and pepper, and serve on a platter.

Asparagus Tart

2 lbs. fresh asparagus, salt and pepper to taste, nutmeg to taste, 4 T butter, ¼ c grated Gruyère cheese, ½ c proscuitto, 3 eggs (beaten), 3 T grated Parmesan cheese

Cook asparagus in boiling salted water until just tender. Cut off tough ends and discard. Chop remaining asparagus into 1 inch pieces and return to pan. Season with salt, pepper, and nutmeg, and add butter. When butter has melted, place in baking pan. Cover with grated Gruyère and proscuitto, and pour beaten eggs over top. Top with Parmesan and cook at medium heat for 30 minutes or until eggs are set.

Fresh Fruit

Florence

The city of Florence, along the edge of Lombardy and Tuscany in northern Italy, was once the heart and soul of the great Italian Renaissance. As a result it is a feast for the senses and a celebration for the spirit—filled to overflowing with some of the greatest art, architecture, and sculpture mankind has ever produced. By the thirteenth century the city was already a hub of resurgent culture and society within medieval Christendom. Blessed with a whole host of great medieval family dynasties—like the Foraboschi and the Uberti, the Farinata and the Guelphs, and of course the Medici—the city became a thriving center of learning, creativity, and achievement. From that day to this, the city has been a primary destination for visitors to Europe. And seldom have the throngs been disappointed: Florence is a treasure trove, the surrounding Tuscan and Lombard countryside is a glory, and the Florentine people are a delight—indeed, the city is almost too good to be true.

Traveling is the ruin of all happiness! There's no looking at a building after seeing Florence.

⊰ FANNY BURNEY (1752–1840) ⊱

Florence is the birthplace of the Renaissance, the soul Italy, and the inspiration of the ages.

⊰ JAMES BONE (1872–1946) ⊱

Oh, their Raphael of the dear Madonnas;
Oh, their Dante of the dread Inferno;
Wrote one song—and in my brain I sing it;
Drew one angel—borne, see, on my bosom.

⊰ ROBERT BROWNING (1812–1889) ⊱

They have a grand mausoleum in Florence, which they built to bury our Lord and Savior and the Medici family in. It sounds blasphemous, but it is true, and here they act blasphemy. The dead and damned Medicis, who cruelly tyrannized over Florence and were her curse for over two hundred years, are salted away in a circle of costly vaults, and in their midst the Holy Sepulchre was to have been set up. The expedition sent to Jerusalem to seize it got into trouble and could not accomplish the burglary, and so the center of the mausoleum is vacant now.

⊰ MARK TWAIN (1835–1910) ⊱

It is the pure white diamond
Dante brought to Beatrice.

           ❧ EUGENE LEE HAMILTON (1845–1907) ❧

Ungrateful Florence! Dante sleeps afar,
Like Scipio, buried by the upbraiding shore.

           ❧ LORD BYRON (1788–1824) ❧

It was pleasant to wake up in Florence, to open the eyes upon a
bright bare room, with a floor of red tiles which look clean though
they are not; with a painted ceiling whereon pink griffins and blue
amorini sport in a forest of yellow violins and bassoons. It was pleasant too, to fling wide the windows, pinching the fingers in unfamiliar fastenings, to lean out into sunshine with beautiful hills and trees
and marble churches opposite, and close below, the Arno, gurgling
against the embankment of the road.

           ❧ E. M. FORSTER (1879–1970) ❧

Although I enter not,
Yet round about the spot
Ofttimes I hover;
And near the Florentine gate,
With longing eyes I wait.

           ❧ WILLIAM MAKEPEACE THACKERAY (1811–1863) ❧

In a dusky café, in the shade of your cap,
Eyes pick out fescoes, nymphs, cupids on their way up.
In a cage, making up for the sour terza-rima crop,
A seedy goldfinch juggles his sharp cadenza.
A chance ray of sunlight splattering the palazzo
And the sacristy where lies Lorenzo
Pierces thick blinds and titillates the veinous
Filthy marble, tubs of snow white verbina;
And the bird's ablaze within his wire Ravenna.

Taking in air, exhaling steam, the doors
Slam shut in Florence. One or two lives one yearns
For (which is up to that faith of yours),
Some night in the first one you learn that love
Doesn't move the stars (or the moon) enough.
For it divides things in two, in half.
Like the cash in your dreams. Like your idle fears
Of dying. If love were to shift the gears
Of southern stars, they'd run to their virgin spheres.

⊶ JOSEPH BRODSKY (1940–1996) ⊷

Summer in Florence has a bad reputation. Florence-wise friends, when told we planned to spend the months of July and August in the city, expressed alarm for our well-being and praise for our courage. But we were altogether undeterred, for we are devoted to the city. It is not any particular building or painting or statue or piazza or bridge, not even the whole unrivaled array of works of art. It is the city itself—the city understood as a self, as a whole, a miraculously developed design.

◦{ R. W .B. Lewis (1917–) }◦

Piazza della Signoria has ere been the political heart of the city
From the Middle Ages to the present day.
It is a singular urbanistic creation that began taking shape
From 1268 onwards,
When the Guelphs gained control of the city yet again
And decided to raze the houses of their rivals
Down, down, down. Down to the very ground.
The first to be destroyed were the towers belonging
To the Foraboschi and the Uberti families,
This in spite of the fact that the head of the former,
The famous Farinata justly celebrated by Dante in his Comedy,
Had defended the city from destruction after its army
Had been disastrously defeated at the battle of Montaperti.
In the end some forty houses were demolished
Which of course, explains
The unusual shape of the square and why
The buildings around it are unaligned.
Nothing was ever to be built on the site again.
Though, the Medicis seemed to take all else as their own.

꿎 GEORGE NATHAN (1888–1971) ꞵ

In Florence may be found,
The heart-light that may abound
Of hope, and truth, and life, and sound
In Christendom's great ground.
        ❧ T. L. GYER (1811–1899) ☙

The city of Dante, of Cosimo de Medici, of Machiavelli, of
Michaelangelo, of Leonardo, and of Vasari: how could it fail to
enchant and delight. Yea, Florence is quite a sight, even in these
dark days of malignant contemporaniety. It is very simply, a civilized
place in the midst of our dull industrial barbarity.
        ❧ FRANCIS GALLATIN (1873–1961) ☙

Magnanimous Florence! How she tends these innocents abroad!
        ❧ MARK TWAIN (1835–1910) ☙

GEOFFREY CHAUCER IN 1372

All too rare is the literary work that completely chronicles an epoch—a work that opens a window on the entirety of a culture: from its art, music, and ideas to its fancies, fables, and foibles. The Canterbury Tales is just such a rarity. But this remarkable work not only described an age, it defined it. Written by Geoffrey Chaucer in the late fourteenth century, the book is a true masterpiece in every sense of the word.

Besides his fascinating insights into the roots and origins of our language, in it, Chaucer gives us a glimpse into the odd nuances of daily life during the halcyon days of the High Middle Ages. He offers us a remarkably enlightened—and thus a surprisingly revisionist—approach to the questions of medieval love, marriage, and family. He affords us a firsthand look at the contemporary sciences, especially astronomy, medicine, psychology, physics, and alchemy. He gives a chronicler's account of the raging social, political, and theological issues of the time. He parodies the social oddities, exults in the cultural profundities, and scrutinizes the civic moralities of his times. He has a genius for capturing the quirks and nuances of ordinary life, the twists and turns of ordinary conversation, and the motivations and inclinations of ordinary people. He expands barnyard fables into cosmic comedies, transforms old wives tales into morality plays, and develops the tidbits of everyday gossip into observations of the universal human condition. As if all that were not enough, he provides us with a fiercely objective analysis of the prevailing Christian worldview of the day. He observed what everyone recognized and recognized what everyone observed. And that is precisely what made him so great.

Thus he painted a vivid portrait of an entire nation—an entire civilization—high and low, male and female, old and young, lay and clerical, learned and ignorant, rogue and righteous, land and sea, town and country, cosmopolitan and provincial—in some of the most beautiful descriptions ever penned and the most compelling plots ever imagined. On any given page you'll find poetry, mythology, history, science, theology, practical ethics, biography, linguistics, art, geography, music, and philosophy—all rendered in a rollicking good story line brimming over with mystery, adventure, romance, and good humor.

And he did this in a language that was hardly usable until he used it; he did this for a nation that was hardly recognizable until he recognized it.

The book is not a classic because some stuffy old professors in musty ivory towers decreed it so; it is a classic because it is classically good and vitally important. Almost two centuries before Shakespeare was born, Chaucer crafted an immortal work that should be a priority on any Christian's must-read list.

We do not have the kind of literary gossip about Chaucer that

Samuel Johnson could record of John Dryden, Joseph Addison, or Jonathan Swift. We do not have the memorabilia, letters, or diaries that color our remembrances of Walter Scott, Thomas Carlyle, or Isaac Watts. We do not have the careful account of contemporary biographers for Chaucer as we do for John Milton, Alexander Pope, or Matthew Prior. Though we have more primary sources and documentary evidence concerning Chaucer's life than Shakespeare's life, that is hardly saying much.

What we do know is that he was born into an Anglo-Norman family of well-to-do vintners in about 1342. He was educated at St. Paul's Almonry in London and early on was sent to be a page in the household of the Countess of Ulster, who later became the Duchess of Clarence, wife of Lionel, the third son of King Edward III. His star rose as a young and talented courtier and he drew the attention of the famed Duke of Lancaster, John of Gaunt. For the rest of his life, he was a trusted confidant of the royal family, serving as a knight during the Hundred Years War in France, as a Royal Justice of the Peace in Kent, as His Majesty's Comptroller of Customs in London, and as an ambassador to Lombardy among the northern Italian city-states.

It was then that Chaucer first came to Florence. And it was there that his literary visions were awakened. It was there that his native interests in poetry were heightened and focused.

He socialized with Petrarch, came to admire Dante, and was

delighted by Boccaccio. He hobnobbed with the greatest poets and thinkers of the slowly emerging Renaissance. There in the world of the Medicis, in the palaces of the Florentine intelligencia, he discovered a thrilling world of art, music, and ideas that would forever change his worldview and his sense of calling.

Though he gleefully immersed himself in that world of the European literati, he was nevertheless disturbed by the lack of a cohesive English poetic tradition. Indeed, the English had no sense of a distinctive tradition of any kind. The Norman Conquest had essentially smothered the once proud Anglo-Saxon culture, annexing it to the Gallic milieu of the continent. But Chaucer was a patriot. He loved his homeland. All the sights and sounds, the people and peculiarities, the habits and humors of England stirred in him a poetic passion that no other place on earth possibly could.

Moved by a love of hearth and homeland, Chaucer committed himself to literary pursuits as a self-conscious exercise in civil and social correction. Since French was still the official language of England, his decision to work in the colloquial of the common people of the streets and fields was very propitious. Like his contemporary John Wyclif he believed that the future of his beloved realm and its emerging culture of liberty was inextricably tied to its indigenous tongue. While Wyclif worked at translating the Bible, Chaucer undertook the arduous task of translating several of the important medieval works he had encountered in Florence expounding the doctrines of chivalry and amour courtois from Latin, Burgundian, Castilian, Italian, and of course, French. Thus was born—or at the very least, thus was confirmed and established—the English language.

The Canterbury Tales was composed at the end of Chaucer's life. In fact, it was never completed due to his premature death in 1400. It thus represents the full fruit of his greatest and most mature labors. But it also represents the full fruit of his times. And they were remarkable times indeed.

During his lifetime, Chaucer witnessed the end of the Plantagenet dynasty, the beginnings of the conflicts between the House of Lancaster and the House of York, the decline of the Crusades, and the rise of the Reconquesta. He observed the great earliest European naval explorations. He was a key participant in the Hundred Years War. Indeed, his life covered the whole span of time between the defining battles of Crecy, Poitiers, and Agincourt. He survived the wretched horrors of the Black Death—when perhaps a fourth of Europe perished. And he somehow escaped harm during the tumultuous Peasants Revolt—which redefined long-static societal roles forever.

Taken together, the man of the times and the times of the man make for a fascinating work of art. Taken together, they make for a book that defines a people and an age like virtually no other book had before or has since. As G. K. Chesterton asserted, "The Poet is the Maker; he is the creator of a cosmos; and Chaucer is the creator of the whole world of his creatures. He made the pilgrimage; he made the pilgrims. He made all the tales told by the pilgrims. Out of him is all the golden pageantry and chivalry of the Knight's Tale; all the rank and rowdy farce of the Miller's; he told through the mouth of the Prioress the pathetic legend of the Child Martyr and through the mouth of the Squire the wild, almost Arabian romance of Cambuscan. And he told them all in a sustained melodious verse, seldom so continuously prolonged in literature; in a style that sings from start to finish."

Like his Florentine heroes—of the ilk of Dante, Medici, and Machiavelli—he was a masterful creator, for he created both art and reality.

A Florentine Repast

'Twas a resplendent repast, on the order of those civilized Florentine folk.
Aye, and glorious too, as 'twas placatingly sumptuous.

GEOFFREY CHAUCER (1343–1400)

Minestra Del Paradiso

4 eggs (separated), ¼ c dry bread crumbs, ¼ c grated Parmesan cheese, nutmeg, beef stock

Beat egg whites until they are stiff but not dry. Beat yolks lightly and fold into egg whites along with bread crumbs, cheese, and nutmeg. In a large pot bring the beef stock to a boil and drop batter from a teaspoon into the stock to form tiny puffs. Remove from heat and cover the pot. Let stand for 7 to 8 minutes or until dumplings are puffed up and thoroughly cooked.

Court Bouillon

2 stalks celery, with leaves (chopped), parsley, bay leaf, peppercorns, thyme, 1 medium onion (chopped), salt, 2 white-meat fish trimmings, 2 quarts cold water, white wine

Place all the ingredients in a large saucepan. Bring to a boil, lower the heat, and simmer for 25 minutes, uncovered. Strain carefully through a cloth. Cool and use to poach fish.

Classic Chicken

2 to 3 T olive oil, 1 large chopped onion, 1 chopped carrot, 2 chopped stalks celery, 1 chicken (cut up), parsley, 2 leeks, 4 crushed coriander seeds, 4 peppercorns, 1/2 t summer savory, salt, and pepper to taste, 1 c dry white wine, 2 T pine nuts, pounded to a paste, 2 T butter, 2 T flour, 2 T lemon juice, 2 egg yolks, 1/2 c heavy cream, 1 T sweet red wine

Heat the oil in a large pot. Add the onion, carrot, and celery and simmer until soft but not brown. Add chicken, herbs, salt, pepper, white wine, and enough water to cover. Simmer chicken covered until tender, about 45 minutes. Strain off broth, reserving 2 cups.

To make sauce: Pound the pine nuts and add to reserved broth. Heat the butter and add the flour, stirring till lightly browned. Add the broth mixture slowly and stir over low heat until smooth and thickened. Simmer for 15 minutes. Beat egg yolks into cream. Gradually add some hot sauce, stirring constantly. Return to pan and stir until very hot. Add lemon juice. Season to taste. Add wine just before serving.

Abbaccione Al Forno

1 small leg of lamb, 6 cloves garlic, salt, 2 springs rosemary, pepper, 1/2 to 3/4 c olive oil, wine

Remove skin from lamb. Mince garlic. Make several slits in lamb. Crush garlic and combine with salt, rosemary, and pepper. Pound into a paste, adding olive oil gradually to thicken the paste. Put into slits and rub remainder all over lamb. Place in roasting pan and roast for 1 to 1½ hours, basting often with olive oil and wine.

Asparagus Torte

2½ lbs. fresh asparagus, salt and pepper to taste, nutmeg to taste, 3 T butter, ¼ c grated Gruyère cheese, 3 eggs (beaten), 3 T grated Parmesan cheese

Cook asparagus in boiling salted water until just tender. Drain. Cut into 1½-inch pieces, return to pan. Sprinkle with salt, pepper, and nutmeg, add butter. When butter has melted, sprinkle with Gruyère and pour beaten eggs over the top. Top with Parmesan cheese and bake in medium oven (350°) for 30 to 40 minutes.

Lasagne with Cheese and Nuts

1 lb. lasagne noodles, torn into bite-sized pieces, 2 c ricotta cheese, ¼ c pignola nuts, 1 c heavy cream, 3 egg yolks, 2 T sugar, ¼ c currants, salt

Cook noodles in lightly salted water until tender. Drain well. Mix cheese with cream, egg yolks, sugar, currants, and salt. Butter a deep dish. Turn noodles into dish and mix throughly with cheese. Fold in nuts. Sprinkle with sugar and breadcrumb topping. Bake in hot oven for 40 minutes until golden.

Vienna

*V*ienna is the beautiful and historic hub of Central and Eastern Europe—just as it has been for more than a thousand years. Thus, it is an international city unlike any other. London, New York, and Paris all boast diverse and multicultural communities—the legacy of far-flung empires and financial interests. But Vienna's character is drawn from a kind of supra-nationalism unique to Hapsburg domains. Here, Northern Europe meets the Balkans, Western Europe meets the Steppes, and the Alps tumble down toward the Adriatic. Like London's suburbanized imperia, New York's urbanized ethnos, and Paris' domesticated outremer, Vienna serves as a vast roiling mix of peoples and traditions. But instead of being a melting pot, it is more like a cauldron of its famed goulash—deliciously incongruous. Though the ancient and venerable walls were torn down in 1857 in order to make way for a series of boulevards that make up the Ringstrasse, the city center remains fabulously medieval to this day. The home of Mozart, Haydn, Brahms, Strauss, Beethoven, Mahler, and Schubert is best known for its Burgtheater, Opera House, and Lichtentaler, but its skyline is most notably punctuated by the palace marvels of the Hofburg, the Belvedere, and the Schonbrunn arrayed along the mighty Danube. Not surprisingly then, visitors have enjoyed the happy anomalies of this wonderful city for centuries.

To waltz onto the streets of Vienna from anywhere else in the world is to discover the delectable delights of civilization at its finest and surest.

ﻬ KARL OSTBAHN (1922–1989) ﻬ

Picture a city filled with row upon row of magnificent palaces and towering steeples, where the artists and composers of yesteryear have left their mark in a place still rich with culture today, a city which combines all the comforts and luxuries of the modern world with the spirit of the past—this is Vienna. For centuries, it has attracted visitors from all over the world who want to experience its charm and beauty and its continual popularity is proof that they have not been disappointed.

ﻬ JAN WESTERLING (1912–1994) ﻬ

The fragrant Vienna woods and spectacular mountains have always inspired in this city held snug against the Danube, to creative heights unmatched by any other capital in Europe. If my heart, my home, my destiny, were not of another domain, surely, this would be enough for solace, but to sip at the strong coffees and sit in the snug booths of this town forever.

ﻬ BONNIE PRINCE CHARLIE (1720–1788) ﻬ

In 1683 the Turks invaded Vienna for the third time—this time almost succeeding. An army of Hapsburg allies finally expelled the raging Ottomans after a two-month siege of the city. It was said that a local businessman used coffee beans left by the Turks to set up the first public coffeehouse. If that is the case, we may agree with the odd poetic sentiment that war is in fact kind and not cruel. The gift of the coffeehouse, whether of Viennese or of Ottoman origin, is gift enough.

❦ BELEAN COLBERT (1946–) ❧

Endearing Waltz! Imported from the Rhine
Famed for the growth and pedigree of wine,
Long be thine import from all duty free,
And hock itself be less esteemed than thee:
In some few qualities alike—for hock
Improves our cellar—thou our living stock.
The head of hock belongs—thy subtler art
Intoxicates alone the heedless hear:
Through the full veins thy gentler poison swims,
and wakes to wantonness the willing limbs.

❦ LORD BYRON (1788–1824) ❧

Come and trip it as you go
On the light fantastic toe.

&ɩ JOHN MILTON (1608–1674) ɩ&

Vienna is the unparalleled treasure of what remains of Christendom.

&ɩ CHARLES DICKENS (1812–1870) ɩ&

Whoe'er has traveled life's dull round,
Where'er his stages may have been,
May sigh to think he still has found
A warm welcome at the Viennese inn.

&ɩ FRANZ KALMANN (1777–1844) ɩ&

Strange and wonderful characters thrive here. Eccentrics are lovingly cared for. The genuine Viennese are thus hardly threatened with
extinction. The bad-tempered, devious, loyal, and charming may yet
be found in the Brunnenmarkt in Ottakring, the Viktor-Adler-Markt
in Favoriten, or in the Naschmarkt, which stretches across the Wien
tributary starting at the Karlsplatz, flanked by gold-decorated Otto
Wagner houses.

&ɩ ABRAHAM KUYPER (1837–1920) ɩ&

Upon Stephansdomplatz, the chapel of Magdalene has burned,
And the Roman ditch, the Graben has been filled,
And in their place stands the horrid Haas House,
Its crenellated glass façade mocking and feigning
All that is good and right and just and true.
Alas, Vienna, is there nothing sacred upon this sacred ground?

❧ JAMES STUART KILMANY (1866–1939) ☙

The Danube rolls along its ceaseless coursing,
With serious architectural angels adding eloquence,
Yet no sum upon an Easter morn is reinforcing
The rout of a folly's progression or its evidence.

So potent is the spell that none decoyed
Remember maidens who danced along its quay
Vienna's long carousal would have toyed
With the magic of motion dangerously on the way.

❧ EMMERICH VON SUPPE (1796–1862) ☙

Reason that is sore progressive, instinct that is sure complete;
Swift passion that now leaps; slow notions that slowly climb.
These are the anthems, the pennons of old Vienna:
Ne'er waiver.
Ne'er suffer the cause.
Ne'er do well by wrong.
Ne'er do wrong by right.
Ne'er again.

❧ WILLIAM YOUNG (1699–1772) ☙

Ah, the Viennese, born high, mighty, and fine,
Content their wealth, and culture their guard,
In action simply just, in conscience clear,
By guilt untainted, undisturbed by fear,
Their means substantial, but their wants but few.
Labor their business, and pleasure too,
Enjoying more comforts in a single hour
Than ages give the wretch condemned to power.

❧ ALBAN WEBERN (1888–1947) ☙

It was in the year 1192 that Richard the Lionhearted was kidnapped whilst on his homeward journey following the third great Crusade to the Holy Land. The jealous Viennese duke who absconded with the great man, held King Richard to ransom for two long years. Some of the ransom money was eventually used to build new city walls. Interestingly, it was upon those very walls that Sulieman laid siege and assault some five centuries later. Thus, after a roundabout fashion, King Richard actually saved Christendom twice from the menace of Islam's conquering Ji'had—proving once again the Scriptural dictum that one may yet speak though dead.

ᴏ⊦ TREVOR LLOYD-MEANS (1893–1978) ⊦ᴏ

ABRAHAM KUYPER IN 1876

Exhausted from his Herculean labors as a journalist, educator, statesman, theologian, pastor, and social reformer, Abraham Kuyper came to visit Vienna shortly after his first term in the Dutch parliament had come to an end. Even as it does today, the city presented him with a jumble of contradictory impressions. The railways, roads, and hotels were all marked by the kind of new world efficiency that was the hallmark of emerging modernity but the food, drink, and music were all marked by the kind of old-world hospitality that was the hallmark of fading antiquity. It was a seductive place with its magnificent theaters, its resplendent palaces, and its broad, bustling boulevards.

Needing rest, Kuyper relaxed in the famous coffeehouses and sidewalk cafés. He feasted on the sagging boards of sausages, strudels, goulashes, and schnitzels at the ornate Biedermeier inns and reveled in the lagers, porters, and stouts at the lively hofbraus. He ambled along the Ringstrasse and listened to the street musicians as he sat in the Burggarten and the Stadtpark. He took particular pleasure in watching the passing parade of busy and cosmopolitan Viennese shopkeepers in the early mornings. He visited the great State Opera House, culled the vast library collection of the Hofburg National Bibliothek, and marveled at the shows in the Spanish Riding School at the Hapsburg palace.

But Kuyper quickly discovered that the one place where all the strains of Vienna's wide-ranging heritage was most evident was the gem that dominated the center of the Stephansdomplatz: St. Stephen's Church, the city's beautiful Gothic cathedral. It was there that he found the reinvigorating vision that he would need for the arduous work that lay ahead of him in years to come.

Consecrated as a Romanesque basilica in 1147, the church has endured the tumult of war, fire, plague, revolution, conquest, and imperial ambition. Over the years, vast Gothic towers, chapels, vaults, spires, and portals were added in a wild variety of architectural textures and scales. Yet in the end, they all seemed to harmonize with one another beautifully. Though conceived quite separately, they appeared to coalesce into an inconsonant unity.

Kuyper was born in 1837, just seven years after Belgium and the Netherlands separated. Though his pious family background, quiet rural community, and meager local schooling combined to afford him only very humble resources, he was a bright student and was early on marked for great things. He attended the university at Leiden and quickly demonstrated an aptitude for serious scholastic work. Following his postgraduate work, he pastored a succession of churches—first in Beesd, then in Utrect, and finally in Amsterdam. He became the leader of the theological conservatives who were working hard to hold at bay the encroachments of modernists and liberals.

By 1872, he had begun publishing a daily newspaper, *De Standaard*. He was already the editor of the inspirational monthly magazine, *De Heraut*. In addition, he had founded a new legal organization to protect the concerns of private Christian schools and had spearheaded the reorganization of the political conservatives into the Anti-Revolutionary Party. He was elected to the lower assembly and quickly became the leading exponent and spokesman for spiritual orthodoxy, fiscal restraint, and judicial tradition. As if all these activities were not enough, he continued the serious academic research he had begun at the university; wrote a flurry of books, pamphlets, and broadsides; and managed a heavy speaking schedule at home and abroad. In later years, he would also establish the Free University of Amsterdam, give vision and direction to the new Dutch Reformed Church, and lead a coalition government as the prime minister. He was a genuine renaissance man in every respect.

It is no wonder then that he was exhausted by the end of 1874. Driven by the obvious need for reform and burdened by the sense of his own leadership role in that great task, he was unflagging in his labors. But of course, he could not single-handedly make the cultural and spiritual changes that were necessary to restore the Netherlands to the balance he so desired—however determined and forceful his efforts were.

When he visited the great old church at the center of Vienna's old city center in 1876, he was somehow reminded of the nature of the

Body of Christ—the eternal church, not made of bricks and mortar. The topsy-turvy adventure that the Gospel inevitably spawns among believers was as oddly paradoxical to him as that ancient structure—but not just because it was improbably diverse yet singularly unified. It was because the whole feat of beauty and balance was actually achieved by anonymous, ordinary people.

Certainly the imperial House of Hapsburg employed a few master craftsmen from time to time over the years to complete one fantastic project or another in the cathedral. But the vast majority of the construction was undertaken by the faithful members of the congregation. Like most of the other great Gothic architectural wonders throughout Europe, the Stephansdomplatz was built by the folks of the town. There were virtually no professional artisans. There were practically no renowned architects. There were no corporate contractors, no certified engineers, and no planning commissions. That feat of stupendous architectural beauty was accomplished by the simple men and women at hand. The extraordinary was achieved by the ordinary.

That, Kuyper realized, was actually the great lesson of all of history. It has always been ordinary people who ultimately were the ones to shape the outcome of great human events—not kings and princes, not masters and tyrants. It has always been laborers and workmen, cousins and acquaintances, who have upended the expectations of the brilliant and the glamorous, the expert and the meticulous. It has been plain folks, simple people, who have literally changed the course of history—because they were the stuff of which history was made. They were the ones who made the world go round.

Staring up at the amazing vaulted ceiling, along the dancing transepts, he was able to recognize anew that most of the grand, glorious headline-making events through the ages have been little more than backdrops to the real drama of green grocers, village cobblers, next door neighbors, and grandfathers. Despite all the hype, hoopla, and hysteria of sensational turns of events, the ordinary people who tended their gardens and raised their children and perfected their trades and minded their businesses were the ones who made or broke a culture. Just like they always had been. Just like they always would be.

Whether building cathedrals like the Stephansdomplatz, toppling the evil empires of the revolutionary modernists, or establishing justice, mercy, and humble faith in his poor fallen homeland, he came to appreciate once again the fact that all of history's most significant developments had been wrought by babushkas and bourgeoisie, shopkeepers and students, dads and daughters, peasants and populists.

Intellectuals and elitists had always been loathe to admit it—and perhaps always would be—but the accomplishments of the quiet and the unsung actually outstripped the loudly publicized deeds of the rich and the regarded. Those who wrote the histories and steered the cultural apparatus were wont to regard the gifts of ordinary people with scorn, but they were in the end sure to be overwhelmed by the torrent of truth evident in God's good providence in the coursing of time.

Kuyper was suddenly refreshed with the notion that it was precisely that irony which enabled the Christian worldview to stand out so brilliantly against the gray dullness of modern thought—it was brilliant because it was so mundane. The Christian faith had always acknowledged that a community's strength was not in its leaders—it was in its followers. It had always recognized that the real decision-makers in any culture were the anonymous plodders who were secretly the heroes of history by virtue of their consistent attention to the details that actually mattered—enjoying their wives, loving their children, helping their neighbors, worshipping in Spirit and in truth, seeking righteousness, and applying their unique gifts to the affairs of everyday life. Thus, he realized, the masters of the universe were not muscle-bound Greek gods come down from Olympus. They were ordinary folks—believers like you and me.

The great task of cultural renewal that he had set before himself appeared at first glance to be a part of the repertoire of the especially skilled, the uniquely prepared, and the remarkably qualified. It looked and sounded hard—like some unscalable summit of spiritual heights. It appeared to be attainable only for the select few, the elite, and the privileged. Like some kind of spiritual juggling act or devotional gymnastics, it seemed to be an ideal for the fit, the ambitious, and the talented.

But nothing could be further from the truth. And Kuyper now realized how it was that he had exhausted himself. Like the building of cathedrals, the great task of cultural renewal was peculiarly the domain of the ordinary. The simplest people doing the simplest things had always been the profoundest course to achieve the profoundest things.

Once he understood that, he was finally able to actually do it. Before his death in 1920, he had successfully mobilized the ordinary citizens of the great Dutch nation to do the difficult work of societal transformation. He was largely able to achieve his aims only after he was disabused of his ability to achieve them.

AUSTRIAN SUPPER

Part of the delight of travel is the variety of food one finds the world over—I am particularly fond of the Austrian suppertime feast.

ABRAHAM KUYPER (1837–1920)

Asparagus Cream Soup

4 lbs. beef soup meat, celery, leek, carrots, shallots, garlic to taste, salt, peppercorns, bay leaf, thyme to taste, 2 lge. bunches asparagus, cut into 2-in. pieces, 1 c heavy cream, 3 egg yolks, 1 sm. bunch parsley

Boil meat in 1 gallon of water. Add celery, leek, carrots, shallots, and seasonings and simmer for about 4 hours. Cook asparagus in a saucepan with water barely to cover for 10 minutes. Add asparagus to beef soup mixture. In a bowl mix the cream with egg yolks and beat together. Take ½ c soup and mix egg and cream mixture into it. Pour back into soup, strain through sieve. Serve garnished with parsley.

Chateaubriand

1 chateaubriand (5 lb.), Bordelaise Sauce

Place meat on a rack in a pan, fat side up, in oven preheated to 500°. Immediately reduce to medium and roast uncovered for 2 hours. Set aside to rest while preparing sauce. Slice and serve with Bordelaise Sauce.

Bordelaise Sauce

½ c dry red wine, 5 crushed black peppercorns, ¼ c beef drippings, ¼ c flour, 1 c tomato purée, ¼ c poached beef marrow, 1 t lemon juice, 1 t chopped parsley, 1 t crushed thyme

In a pot cook red wine and peppercorns until slightly reduced, then add beef drippings, flour, and tomato purée. Simmer for 10 minutes. Add beef marrow and lemon juice. Reduce until thickened. Add parsley and thyme.

Sautéed New Potatoes

3 T clarified butter, 2 doz. tiny new potatoes (scrubbed well), salt

Heat butter in a heavy saucepan. Add potatoes and cook slowly until tender. Shake the pan occasionally. Drain and serve with salt to taste.

Hot Bread

Sachertorte

3/4 c butter (softened), 3/4 c sugar, 6 oz. melted semisweet chocolate, 8 egg yolks, pinch salt, 8 egg whites, 1 t vanilla extract, 1 1/4 c flour, 1/2 c apricot preserves, 4 c sugar, 2 T corn syrup, 1 1/3 c cold water, 2 oz. melted semisweet chocolate, 2 T Cognac

Cream together butter and 3/4 c sugar until light. Add the 6 oz. melted chocolate and mix well. Beat in egg yolks one at a time, mixing well after each addition. Add salt. Beat egg whites until stiff. Add vanilla to whites. Fold one third of the egg whites into batter. Fold flour into batter, alternating with remaining egg whites. Pour into a 10-inch greased springform pan. Bake in medium oven (350°) about 40 minutes. Cool overnight. Spread with apricot preserves.

Put sugar, corn syrup, and water in a heavy pan and stir over low heat until sugar is melted. Cover and cook on low heat for 5 minutes. Remove cover and boil uncovered for 5 minutes, reaching soft ball stage. Remove from heat and pour onto a marble slab. When cool enough to handle, work it with a spatula, scraping and folding. Knead until smooth. Allow to stand at room temperature overnight, covered with a damp cloth. Soften 1 c fondant in a double boiler. Add the 2 oz. melted semisweet chocolate and 2 T Cognac. Pour fondant onto cake and rotate cake to spread icing over preserves.

New York

Considered by many to be the single greatest city in the world, New York is a marvel to behold—and it always has been, it seems. From its earliest days in the seventeenth century as a Dutch settlement and its British colonial ascendancy to its early American prominence and its current status as an international cultural and business center, the city has always aspired to larger than life pretensions of glory and visions of grandeur. And, by all accounts, it has essentially achieved them. It is surprisingly compact yet absurdly gargantuan. It is unique unto itself yet wildly varied. It is a jumble of contradictions, yet carefully organized and codified. It is a world city that no land can entirely claim as its own, but it is, as a result, steadfastly American. It is a kind of towering Babel where, nevertheless, every nation, tribe and tongue has found a way to cohabit peacefully—at least, somewhat peacefully.

New York is a place halfway between America and the world.
    ❧ GEORGE BERNARD SHAW (1856–1950) ☙

New York is to the nation what the white church spire is to the village—the visible symbol of aspiration and faith, the white plume saying the way is up!
    ❧ E. B. WHITE (1899–1985) ☙

What is barely hinted at in other cities is condensed and enlarged in New York.
    ❧ SAUL BELLOW (1915–) ☙

Dwarfed by their vast monoliths of glass and steel
New Yorkers bustle unconcerned and unaware,
Their hive of activity though bound in captivity real
Is hardly an issue in their magnificent Vanity Fair.
    ❧ TRISTAN GYLBERD (1954–) ☙

Everyone ought to have a Lower East Side in their life.
    ❧ IRVING BERLIN (1888–1989) ☙

One belongs to New York instantly. One belongs to it as much in five minutes as in five years.

ᚥ THOMAS WOLFE (1900–1938) ᚥ

No one should come to New York unless he is willing to be lucky.

ᚥ E. B. WHITE (1899–1985) ᚥ

New York City will be a great place if they ever finish it.

ᚥ O. HENRY (1862–1910) ᚥ

All of everything is concentrated here, population, theater, art, writing, publishing, importing, business, murder, mugging, luxury, poverty. It's all of everything. It goes all night. It is tireless and its air is charged with energy.

ᚥ JOHN STEINBECK (1902–1968) ᚥ

It has long been recognized that America was an asylum. But in New York it sometimes rather looks to be a bit of a lunatic asylum.

ᚥ G. K. CHESTERTON (1874–1936) ᚥ

Performances, assortments, resumés,
Up Times Square to Columbus Circle lights,
Channel the congresses, the nightly sessions,
Refractions of the thousand theater faces:
Mysterious kitchens; You shall search them all.

Some day by heart you'll learn each famous sight
And watch the curtain lift in hell's despite;
You'll find the garden in the third act dead,
Finger your knees—and wish yourself in bed
With tabloid crime sheets perched in easy sight.

Then let you reach your hat
And go.
As usual, let you—also
Walking down—exclaim
To twelve upward leaving
A subscription praise
For what time slays.

Or can't you quite make up your mind to ride;
A walk is better underneath the L a brisk
Ten blocks or so before? But you find yourself
Preparing a penguin flexions of the arms,
As usual you will meet the scuttle yawn:
The subway yawns the quickest promise home.

Be minimum, then, to swim the hiving swarms
Out of the Square, the Circle burning bright;
Avoid the glass doors gyring at your right,
Where boxed alone a second, eyes take fright,
Quite unprepared rush naked back to light:
And down beside the turnstile press the coin
Into the slot. The gongs already rattle.

And so
Of cities you bespeak
Subways, rivered under streets
And rivers; in the car
The overtone of motion
Underground, the monotone
Of motion is the sound
Of other faces, also underground.

❦ HART CRANE (1899–1932) ❧

New York is as Latin as any of the great Latin American capitals.
◦{ JORGES BORGES (1899–1986) }◦

I love New York. It is so Irish.
◦{ FLAN O'BRIEN (1911–1966) }◦

New York is as Italian as Rome is—perhaps even more so.
◦{ UMBERTO ECO (1929–) }◦

New York is nearly as Jewish as Jerusalem.
◦{ DAVID BEN-GURION (1886–1973) }◦

When I had looked at the lights of Broadway by night, I made to my American friends an innocent remark that seemed for some reason to amuse them. I had looked, not without joy, at the long kaleido-scope of colored lights arranged in large letters and sprawling trade-marks, advertising everything, from pork to pianos, through the agency of the two most vivid and most mystical gifts of God: color and fire. I said to them in my simplicity: What a glorious garden of wonders this would be, to anyone who was lucky enough to be unable to read.
◦{ G. K. CHESTERTON (1874–1936) }◦

New York is a catastrophe—but a magnificent catastrophe.
◦{ LE CORBUSIER (1887–1965) }◦

New York City is absolutely and wretchedly awful. Yet it remains somehow triumphant and thus absolutely glorious in its wretched awfulness.

JOHN RUSKIN (1819–1900)

New York City's unique and defining charm is that it offers a dazzling variety of everything—a cultural smorgasbord for the entire globe. Manhattan is a small, precious stretch of land that runs only 13 miles long and is less than three miles wide yet it is home to 1.5 million people and host to over four million daily commuters. The population of Manhattan exceeds the populations of Vermont and Wyoming combined, and it comprises only 22.6 square miles. Including all of the city's five boroughs, New York's population is approximately 7.3 million. Manhattan has used more marble in churches, building lobbies, and facades than all of Rome. It boasts as many French restaurants as Paris. It offers more museums and art galleries than London and has over one thousand skyscrapers—more than any other city in the world.

KIM TAYLOR (1960–)

New York is a cosmopolitan city, but it is not a city of cosmopolitans. Most of the masses in New York have a nation whether or not it be the nation to which New York ostensibly belongs. They are exiles or they are citizens; there is no moment when they are cosmopolitans. But very often the exiles bring with them not only rooted traditions, but rooted truths.

        G. K. CHESTERTON (1874–1936)

Purple-robed and pauper-clad,
Raving, rotting, money-mad;
A squirming herd in Mammon's mesh,
A wilderness of human flesh;
Crazed with avarice, lust, and rum,
New York, thy name's Delirium.

        BYRON RUFUS NEWTON (1861–1938)

There's only one Big Apple. That's New York.

        JOHN FITZGERALD (1863–1950)

I'm sick o' New York City an' the roarin' o' the thrains
That rowl above the blesed roofs an' undernaith the dhrains;
Wid dust an' smoke an' divilmint I'm moidhered head and brains,
An' I'm thinkin' o' the skies of ould Kilkinny!

        JAMES DOLLARD (1872–1951)

City, lyric city:

City kind to actresses; tolerant of actors; city of independent hand-maidens. City of contraceptions, contraptions, and curses thundered from a thousand pulpits. City of unfortunate fortune tellers. City entered by night.

Reporters cover you, yet you are never covered.

City of carpenters without wood, of plumbers without mercy. City of uncomfortable comfort stations. City of clanging radiators, of supine superintendents. City wherein there is no room to die.

City wrought in flame. City of arguments unending. City of terminals, city of endings, city of the last attempt. City wherein no one knows whether he is coming or going. City of odalisques working in stores, of seraglios seeking for sultans, of tired old women scrubbing offices by night. Great glorious patriotic city, giving its canes to crippled soldiers. Fairy city in those magic hours of the passing night; the pause before the dawn.

Dress suit city, for hire and for keeps.

City that breathes of things too large for books, that is too beautiful for poets, too terrible for drama, too true for testimony.

City worth visiting, if only for a week.

ᴥ FELIX RIESENBERG (1879–1949) ᴥ

I love New York.

ᴥ ED KOCH (1924–) ᴥ

ALEXIS DE TOCQUEVILLE IN 1831

Much has changed in New York since the two-week-long visit of Alexis de Tocqueville and Gustav de Beaumont in 1831. They described the city then as a rather disagreeable provincial town with badly paved roads, garish arts, teeming confusion, pretentious architecture, and bizarrely rude manners. While some critics might well still make the such charges against the city, clearly New York has come of age in the interval between then and now.

The two aristocratic travelers were at the beginning of what would be a nine-month-long tour of the fledgling United States. They had an official mandate from the French government to study the land's criminal justice system—but they were actually interested in seeing far more than America's courts and jails. They wanted to explore the essence of the American spirit, discover the secret to American ingenuity, and plumb the depths of the American soul. Eventually, they would visit nineteen of the country's then twenty-four states, stopping in more than fifty towns and villages from the thronging urban centers of the east to the rough and tumble frontier settlements of the west. They covered more than eight thousand miles, mostly by foot, on horseback, in steamboats, and on stage coaches. As de Tocqueville later wrote, "I confess that in America, I saw more than America; I sought there the image of democracy itself, with its inclinations, its character, its prejudices, and its passions, in order to learn what we have to fear or to hope from its progress."

New York was the young republic's thriving banking and trading center. Though it had spread across only about half of Manhattan Island—the rest was still divided between country estates, a few farms, and even a bit of wild forest land—the city had already become densely populated and was growing rapidly. It was shot through with the great American optimism of the Jacksonian Age. It was already the nation's largest city, and it hummed with commerce. Of course, there was no Empire State Building, no Statue of Liberty, no Times Square, no Central Park, no Radio City Music Hall, and no Rockefeller Center—each of these New York landmarks would come in succeeding years. Nevertheless, much of what would ultimately give the city its unique character and culture was already in evidence.

Immigrants, for instance, comprised a large proportion of the city's population. Bringing with them the exotic foods, traditions, and cultures of their homelands, they added an international flavor to New York that persists to this day. In addition, the unique admixture of rich and poor, so much a part of the character of the city today—in contrast to the very strict socioeconomic stratification and segmentation of most other great cities—was already a distinctive part of the New York experience. The famous French travelers were amazed—as are so many right up to the present.

Alexis de Tocqueville was born into the aristocracy in 1805, during the halcyon days of the Napoleonic Empire. His family had suffered much during the French Revolution—as had so many of noble birth. But Napoleon restored their fortunes. As a result, de Tocqueville was able to enjoy a privileged upbringing despite all the vicissitudes of the time. As a young adult, he served the ever-changing French governing institutions—thus preserving his family's lands and fortune.

He was intellectually precocious, and demonstrated great ability early on. As a result of his interests in the rising tide of worldwide bourgeois capitalism and its relation to republican institutions, he was made a commissioner of the new constitutional monarchy which had been swept into power the previous year. With the vocal support of King Louis Philippe and his cabal of bourgeois advisors—including the venerable nobleman, Marquis de Lafayette, the esteemed soldier, Jean Lafitte, and the renowned historian, Francois-Pierre Guillaume Guizot—he was elevated to the highest strata of French society and life.

He was impressed by the warren of crooked little streets in Greenwich Village and Lower Manhattan. He was amazed at the foresight of the city grid laid out for the northern extremities of Midtown. He was ingratiated by the hospitality of the nouveau riche who inhabited the large river estates along the Hudson. And he was fascinated by the frenetic energy of the average New Yorker, immigrant and native-born alike.

He attributed this remarkable dynamism to the freedom they seemed to enjoy, indeed, even thrive upon. He wrote, "Here freedom is unrestrained, and subsists by being useful to everyone without injuring anybody. There is something undeniably feverish in the activity it imparts to industry and to the human spirit." It was an observation that he would recall again and again as he traveled throughout the land—but it was especially evident in his visit to New York.

Though the city was then under the control of a handful of politicians led by Martin van Buren—its seems the city has always had its machines from Aaron Burr's Chase Manhattan clique to Boss Tweed's Tammany Ring—it was marked by a persistent independence of heart, soul, mind, and spirit. This was, to de Tocqueville, the greatest landmark of the already amazing New York City profile.

When he returned to France, de Tocqueville sat down to document his experiences and to sort through his conclusions. Eventually, he published his observations in a massive two volume work entitled *The Republic of the United States of America*—later retitled *Democracy in America* by American liberal academics. The book became an instant classic. It helped to explain the American phenomenon to Europeans. But it also provided a rare objective look at the culture of America for Americans. And his discoveries were thus woven into the mythos and the consciousness of thoughtful men and women the world over. Many historians believe that it was the way de

Tocqueville articulated those discoveries that provided the philosophical paradigm shift necessary for the ultimate American triumph and the advent of the American century.

Essentially what he discovered was that America was the only modern nation in the world that was founded on a creed. Other nations found their identity and cohesion in ethnicity, geography, partisan ideology, or cultural tradition. But America was founded on certain ideas—ideas about freedom, human dignity, and social responsibility. It was this profound peculiarity that most struck him. He called it "American exceptionalism."

He simultaneously concluded that if their great experiment in liberty and their extraordinary American exceptionalism were to be maintained over the course of succeeding generations, then an informed patriotism would have to be instilled in the hearts and minds of the young. Not surprisingly then, de Tocqueville has oft been quoted—perhaps apocryphally, but nevertheless true to the basic tenets of his evident opinion—saying: "I sought for the greatness and genius of America in her commodious harbors and her ample rivers, and it was not there; in her fertile fields and boundless prairies, and it was not there; in her rich mines and her vast world commerce, and it was not there. Not until I went to the churches of America and heard her pulpits aflame with righteousness did I understand the secret of her genius and power. America is great because she is good and if America ever ceases to be good, America will cease to be great."

His remarkable chronicle was offered in the hope that the ideas that made America both great and good might remain the common currency of the national life. He felt that the world needed to know those things—because the world needed to share those things.

New York was the starting place of de Tocqueville's great journey—both physical and intellectual. It was there that he first observed all that was right and all that was wrong with America. It was there that he first caught a glimpse of liberty's great power, great promise, and great purpose. It was also there that he first felt the gnawing certainty that something so great could greatly disappoint.

The more things change, the more they stay the same.

NEW YORK LUNCHEON

The vast equality of democracy extends even to the luncheon table.
ALEXIS DE TOCQUEVILLE (1805–1859)

Game Hens with Winter Vegetables and Chestnuts

1 bell pepper, olive oil, 1 c ½-inch cubes peeled acorn squash, 1 c peeled and quartered white potatoes, 1 c stringed green beans (cut into 1-inch lengths), 4 Cornish game hens (quartered with backs removed), salt and pepper, 1 c chopped mushrooms, 2 dozen roasted chestnuts, 2 c chicken stock, ½ c melted butter, 2 T chopped fresh thyme, 8 c chopped spinach

In a skillet sauté bell pepper in olive oil. In a pan cook squash and potatoes in boiling salted water 10 minutes. Add green beans and cook 10 minutes. Drain. Add onions to vegetable mixture. Set aside. Heat 1 T oil in heavy Dutch oven over medium-high heat. Season game hens with salt and pepper. Add each hen to Dutch oven and cook until browned on all sides and almost cooked through, turning often. Each hen will take about 15 minutes. Set hens aside. Lower heat to low medium. Add mushrooms to Dutch oven and sauté 4 minutes. Stir in vegetable mixture and chestnuts. Place hens on top of vegetable mixture in Dutch oven. Whisk together chicken stock, melted butter, and thyme. Pour liquid mixture over hens in pot. Cover and simmer another 30 minutes. Transfer game hens to serving plates. Salt and pepper to taste. Divide vegetables among plates.

Creamed Onions

*8 medium unpeeled onions, ¹/₄ c melted butter, 2 T flour, bay leaf,
¹/₄ c sherry, ¹/₄ c chopped parsley, ¹/₄ t paprika, ¹/₂ t nutmeg*

In a double boiler over boiling water, cook onions for 30 minutes.
Peel onions and keep warm. While onions are steaming, make cream
sauce. To 2 T melted butter, add flour. Stir milk in slowly. Add bay
leaf, sherry, and parsley. When thickened, pour over onions and
sprinkle with paprika.

Serve with hot yeast rolls.

Steamed Caramel Pudding

*¹/₂ c sugar, 1 c hot milk, 2 T butter, 5 eggs, 1 t vanilla, 1¹/₂ T flour, 1 c
ground walnuts or almonds*

Melt sugar in a heavy skillet. When it is light brown, stir in the
hot milk. Set aside. In a medium bowl beat butter with whisk until
soft, adding the eggs one at a time. Add the milk/sugar mixture,
vanilla, flour, and nuts. Beat batter until smooth. Pour into a greased
pudding mold. Cover well and steam over low heat for 1 hour.

Washington

*T*he capital of the greatest democracy on earth is a gleaming city of stately monuments, classic public buildings, broad boulevards, and verdant parks. Carefully designed by Pierre L'Enfant and meticulously laid out by Andrew Ellicott at the end of the eighteenth century, the city is arranged according to a gridiron of streets cut by diagonal avenues radiating from the Mall that runs between the Capitol and the White House. Situated on the banks of the Potomac River, the city was until the advent of the twentieth century a rather remote and inaccessible outpost of urbanity amidst distinctly rural surroundings. Despite its lofty architecture and natural beauty, the city is inescapably linked to the rough and tumble world of politics—as most of its visitors have been only too quick to point out. Thus, the resplendent sights and sites are often forced to take a back seat to the litigious cites and slights of partisanism.

Washington is a city of Southern efficiency and Northern charm.
ᴏʃ JOHN F. KENNEDY (1917–1963) ʃᴏ

What a magnificent view the city begets
When the cherry blossoms bloom
It is almost enough to make one forget
What it is that these politicians do.
ᴏʃ TRISTAN GYLBERD (1954–) ʃᴏ

To walk the length of the Mall, with the great spire of the
Washington Monument in sight, the Smithsonian to the left, the
National Gallery to the right, Capitol Hill before, and the White
House aft, is to recall both the greatness of this land and the ease
with which we tend to slip into deleterious complacency—for here
are the memorials to our glorious past and our mediocre present,
our patriotic legacy and our political abdication. Object lessons, all.
ᴏʃ HERBERT LARSSEN (1887–1962) ʃᴏ

The architecture is monumental
As befits this great city, Capital of this great land.
The bustle about the streets is frenetic
As betokens its great energy, its great affairs.
The aura of power is palpable
As expected in its great cauldron, its great ire.
Yet somehow it all disappoints:
As if America were actually elsewhere;
As if America were absent from this, her Seat.

        JAMES STUART KILMANY (1866–1939)

Fellow citizens! Clouds and darkness are round about Him. His pavilion is dark waters and thick clouds of the skies. Justice and judgment are the establishment of His throne. Mercy and truth shall go before His face. Fellow citizens! God reigns, e'en o'er the government in Washington—despite all appearances.

        JAMES A. GARFIELD (1831–1881)

In this town you don't write anything that you can phone, you don't phone anything that you can talk face to face, you don't talk anything face to face that you can smile, you don't smile anything that you can wink, and you don't wink anything that you can nod.

        EARL LONG (1895–1960)

If you want a friend in Washington, buy a dog.

⊶ HARRY TRUMAN (1884–1972) ⊷

It is often so with institutions already undermined: they are at their most splendid external phase when they are ripe for downfall.

⊶ HILAIRE BELLOC (1870–1953) ⊷

The first thing you learn when you come to Washington is that no party is as bad as its leaders.

⊶ WILL ROGERS (1879–1935) ⊷

In Washington, the surest way to stop any transaction of business and split the ranks of the sundry political forces is to simply appeal to a principle. The only men with convictions in this town are just out on parole.

⊶ JAMES LEE OTIS (1919–1977) ⊷

Being in politics in Washington is like being a football coach; you have to be smart enough to understand the game, and dumb enough to think it's important.

⊶ EUGENE MCCARTHY (1916–1996) ⊷

It ought to be a majestic sight to behold:
This seat of power, this treasury of wealth, this safeguard of liberty,
this emblem of freedom.
Alas, it is lamentable that such sacred resources are entrusted
To such a banal city of corruption, greed, and hubris
Filled to over-brimming with callous, petty, and conniving, as
indeed, Washington is.

ᴏᶠ TRISTAN GYLBERD (1954–) ᶠᴏ

Is there any place more ironic on all the earth than this, the capital
of human freedom, the symbol of human lechery?

ᴏᶠ BOOKER T. WASHINGTON (1856–1915) ᶠᴏ

My God! What is there in this place that a man should ever want to
get into it?

ᴏᶠ JAMES GARFIELD (1831–1881) ᶠᴏ

A little shallop floating slow along
The fair Potomac's tide,
The oarsman pausing for a simple song,
Sung softly at his side.

Great boughs of laurel garlanding the boat,
Won from the bloomy store
Of forests, lying purple and remote
Along the eastern shore.

Far off the city and the growing dome
Of the fair Capitol,
White and ethereal as the feathery foam
Fringing the oar-blade's fall.

In the horizon waits one patient star,
A sphere of silver white,
While the moon, above the hill-tops far,
Slow reddens into sight.

ELIZABETH AKERS ALLEN (1842–1898)

There are a number of things wrong with Washington. One of them is that everyone has been too long away from home.
~ DWIGHT D. EISENHOWER (1890–1969) ~

Men generally believe that they get no more from the vast and costly operations of the government in Washington than they get from the money they lend to their loutish in-laws.
~ H. L. MENCKEN (1880–1956) ~

There is no trick to being a humorist when you have the whole government in Washington working for you.
~ WILL ROGERS (1879–1935) ~

If it were not for the government in Washington, we should have nothing left to laugh at.
~ JAMES GARFIELD (1831–1881) ~

If you're going to sin, sin against God, not the bureaucracy in Washington. God will forgive you but the bureaucracy won't.
~ HYMAN RICKOVER (1900–1986) ~

Bureaucracy is the technical embodiment of hell itself.

◆ C. S. LEWIS (1898–1963) ◈

Bureaucracy is the greatest threat to freedom and liberty conceived by man.

◆ ALEXIS DE TOCQUEVILLE (1805–1859) ◈

Here richly, with ridiculous display
The politician's corpse was laid away
While all his acquaintance sneered and slanged,
I wept; for I had longed to see him hanged.

◆ HILAIRE BELLOC (1870–1953) ◈

The most healing of medicines, unduly administered, becomes the most deadly of poisons. That is a lesson all too evident to every visitor to our nation's capital.

◆ JOHN QUINCY ADAMS (1767–1848) ◈

It is perhaps a universal rule, but it is especially true in Washington: do-gooders are the world's most notorious do-baders.

◆ TRISTAN GYLBERD (1954–) ◈

HERMAN MELVILLE IN 1862

When Herman Melville first visited Washington, the nation was in the midst of its terribly uncivil War between the States. The city itself was in an awful state. Even in the best of circumstances, it would have looked dramatically different that it does today—the Washington Monument was not yet built, the Smithsonian Institution was contained in a single small building, the new cast-iron dome for the Capitol had only been partially constructed, and the great parks were rough, unkempt, and untended. The streets were muddy, ill-managed, and clogged with commercial wagons. The government offices were crowded, poorly administered, and badly maintained. And worse, these were hardly the best of circumstances.

Wartime Washington was a awash in the detritus of strife. Melville was shocked by the numbers of wounded soldiers that walked the streets near the Federal hospitals. He was outraged by the sight of the continuing slave trade just blocks from President Lincoln's residence in the White House. And he was baffled by the sense of doom that seemed to pervade every conversation. A goodly number of the citizens—and many of the most prominent leaders—seemed to be gripped by an almost irrational frenzy of fear and trepidation. Indeed, it seemed that the Confederate forces under the able leadership of General Lee and Jackson might sweep across the

Virginia border any day—as they had been threatening to do since the beginning of the armed hostilities—sending the government fleeing into an ignominious exile.

Melville was an eminent man of letters—but he was not visiting Washington as a writer. Rather, he had come as a government official. He worked in New York at the Port Authority as a customs inspector, having given up writing some five years earlier.

Thus, in 1862, both the man and the city were rather out of sorts.

The number of truly masterful American writers can probably be numbered on two hands—Cotton Mather, James Fenimore Cooper, Nathaniel Hawthorne, Washington Irving, Mark Twain, Edgar Allan Poe, Henry Wadsworth Longfellow, Henry Adams, William Faulkner, and of course Herman Melville. Each of these authors achieved great success during their lifetimes and were mourned at their deaths—all except Melville. In fact, he died in his New York City home in 1891 at the age of seventy-two in utter obscurity—his brilliant career and voluminous writings by then long forgotten.

A short obituary appearing the day afterward in the *New York Press* recalled, "Melville had once been one of the most popular writers in the United States," but added, "The later years of his life had been so quiet that probably even his own generation has long thought him dead." Another paper in the city, the *Daily Tribune*, noted, "The deceased had won considerable fame as an author by the publication of a book entitled *Typee*, which was the account of his experience while a captive in the hands of the savages of the Marquesas Islands. This was his first and best work although he later wrote a number of other stories, which were published more for private than public circulation."

The obituaries demonstrate one of the most remarkable ironies in the history of American letters—aside from some early renown as an adventure writer, Melville was a publishing failure. During the eleven short years of his literary activity, he was either misunderstood and miscast, or castigated and ignored. Even so, some of the best fiction ever produced in the English language flowed from his pen—*Moby Dick*, *Billy Budd*, *Redburn*, *The Piazza Tales*, *The Confidence Man*, *White-Jacket*, and *Omoo*. By the time he had reached forty, however, he had abandoned his writing in order to provide for his family.

It was not until some thirty years after his demise that academics rediscovered his genius. They marveled at the richness of his prose, the depth of his characterizations, the complexity of his symbiology, and the passion of his theology. *Moby Dick*, in particular, was widely heralded as a genuine masterpiece, while several of his other works were made the subjects of serious critical acclaim. Soon Melville was deservedly enshrined in the pantheon of literary greatness.

The story Melville conceived as his magnum opus was published after he had attained his minor popularity as a writer of pulp thrillers. But he aspired to something far greater than merely an

intrepid tale of sea adventure. He wanted to write great and endur-
ing literature. Alas, that was hardly the kind of pap that publishers in
the middle of the nineteenth century were looking for. The more
things change, the more they stay the same.

Melville was undeterred, and the big, brash, and boisterous book
he wrote, *Moby Dick*, proved to be a multilayered novel of expansive
scope, subtle intrigue, and stunning exploits. Like much of his writing, the story was constructed as a kind of literary and theological
puzzle. But this surprising and scintillating double-coded
labyrinth—which apparently was intended to follow the thematic
structure of a great Puritan sermon—never obstructed the pace or
the sense of the story. Powerful scenic images and a rip-roaring
series of illusions, cons, ploys, and deceptions gave the book an
immediacy and a page-turning quality generally unknown in serious
literary works. It was, in short, brilliantly conceived and passionately
executed.

Born in 1819, the son of a struggling merchant, Melville had an
adventurous youth—serving on whaling vessels and trading ships
throughout the Pacific and across the Atlantic. His literary career,
such as it was, grew out of a desire to tell of those experiences. His
maturity as a writer blossomed quickly and he was drawn into the
high-brow literary circle that included Longfellow and Hawthorne.
But his unwillingness to compromise either his style or his content
to suit popular tastes doomed his commercial appeal. When he quit

writing altogether in 1857, he asserted that he'd rather lay down his pen than lower his standards: "What I feel most moved to write will not pay. Yet write the other way, I cannot."

Thus, with the force of an unerring moral compunction, he put away his parchments and went to work as an inspector at the busy New York harbor. That kind of uncompromising ethical conviction is readily apparent in *Moby Dick*. The book is an unrestrained expression of originality and verve. But it is also a forceful exertion of will against all odds erupting upon the intellectual stage with a lusty obsession for truth and resolution: "Unconsciously my chirography expands into placard capitals. Give me a condor's quill. Give me Vesuvius's crater for an inkstand."

He wrote of leviathans. Indeed, he was himself a leviathan.

When he visited Washington in 1862, he could not help but see the sad parallels between the squandered promise of his own life and the squandered promise of the national life. Everything that was necessary for greatness in both was everywhere evident, yet the expediencies of the moment and the exigencies of circumstances demanded otherwise.

After his short visit, during which he tended to what he called "the banal administrative chores typical of Washington politics," he returned to his home, saddened by the irony of it all.

CAPITAL BREAKFAST

In the capital, every meal is an opportunity for politics to be displayed, even at breakfast—a most disconcerting notion, I dare say.
HERMAN MELVILLE (1819–1891)

Baked Cheese Grits

4 c water, 1 t salt, 5 T butter, 1 c grits, ½ c grated Cheddar cheese, 4 eggs, ⅓ c milk

In a saucepan bring the water, salt, and butter to a boil. Slowly whisk the grits into the water, and cook until thick. Mix in the cheese. In separate bowl, beat eggs and milk together. Whisk into grits. Bake in a hot oven (375°) for 45 minutes to 1 hour.

Scrambled Eggs

Fried Virginia Ham

Baked Apples

5 medium apples, 4 T butter, ½ c brown sugar, 1 t grated nutmeg, 2 t cinnamon

Slice apples while the butter is heating in a heavy skillet. Place apples in butter. Add the remaining ingredients, stirring often to coat evenly. Cook until tender, but not soft.

Applecake

3 eggs, 1 c sugar, ⅓ c shortening, 1 t vanilla extract, 2 c flour,
3 lge. apples, warm cream

In a large bowl, combine the eggs, sugar, shortening, and vanilla. Fold the flour into the mixture. Set aside. Peel, quarter, and score the apples deeply.

Butter and flour a springform pan. Spoon the thick batter into the pan. Place the apples around the edge of the pan and in the center. Bake in a medium oven (350°) for about 1 hour and 15 minutes. Serve with warm cream.

Hot Coffee

Jerusalem

*L*ike man himself, this city is an enigma. The cradle of civilization, the well-spring of faith, the powderkeg of ardor, and the terminus of time—there is no other place on earth where so much has occurred for so long and affected so many. Jerusalem is the ominous, swarthy, and mysterious hinge upon which, it seems, all of history turns. Alternately rocked by unending wars and soothed by undying devotion, tortured by unflinching fanaticism and calmed by unyielding patience, this small city of sand and stone is now, and always has been, the stage upon which the passion play of mankind's trauma is set—where war is waged for the sake of peace, where hatred is stoked for the sake of righteous-ness, and where tyranny is invoked for the sake of freedom. It has thus always been a compelling destination for visitors—from the days of the festival-goers of ancient Israel to the minions of modern tourism. "Next year in Jerusalem" has been the pledge of hungering, yearning, searching souls for as long as the memory of man can be recalled.

So we part sadly in this troubled world
To meet with joy in sweet Jerusalem.
      WILLIAM SHAKESPEARE (C. 1564–1616)

Jerusalem the golden, with milk and honey blest,
Beneath thy contemplation sink heart and voice oppressed.
      JOHN MASON NEALE (1818–1866)

A fast walker could go outside the walls of Jerusalem and walk
entirely around the city in an hour. I do not know how else to make
one understand how small it is. And the appearance of this tiny city
is peculiar. It is a knobby with countless little domes as a prison door
is with bolt heads.
      MARK TWAIN (1835–1910)

Jerusalem my happy home,
When shall I come to thee?
When shall my sorrows have an end?
Thy joys, when shall I see?

Thy saints are crowned with glory great;
They see God face to face;
They triumph still, they still rejoice:
Most happy is their case.

Jerusalem, Jerusalem,
God grant that I may see
Thine endless joy, and of the same
Partaker ever be.

JOSEPH BROMEHEAD (1767–1822)

I was glad when they said unto me, let us go into the house of the
Lord. Our feet shall stand within thy gates, O Jerusalem. Jerusalem
is builded as a city that is compact together: whither the tribes go
up, the tribes of the Lord, unto the testimony of Israel, to give
thanks to the name of the Lord.

PSALM 122

Comfort, comfort, ye my people,
Speak ye peace, thus saith our God;
Comfort those who sit in darkness,
Mourning 'neath their sorrow's load.
Speak ye to Jerusalem
Of the peace that waits for them;
Tell her that her sins I cover,
And her warfare is now over.

                          JOHANNES OLEARIUS (1649–1697)

At last the march shall end,
The wearied ones shall rest;
The pilgrims find their Father's house
Jerusalem the blest.

                          EDWARD PLUMPTRE (1806–1867)

Surely Jerusalem embodies all that is tender and lovely in the human soul.

                          WILLIAM BLAKE (1757–1827)

Jerusalem represents all that is twisted and malignant in the spirit of man.

of HAVELOCK ELLIS (1859–1939) ȷo

By the waters of Babylon, there we sat down, yea, we wept, when we remembered Zion. We hanged our harps upon the willows in the midst thereof. For there they that carried us away captive required of us a song; and they that wasted us required of us mirth, saying sing us one of the songs of Zion. How shall we sing the Lord's song in a strange land? If I forget thee, O Jerusalem, let my right hand forget her cunning. If I do not remember thee, let my tongue cleave to the roof of my mouth; if I prefer not Jerusalem above my chief joy.

of PSALM 137 ȷo

Jerusalem has been a battleground throughout all time: from Nebuchadnezar to Napoleon, from the Ottomans to the Ayatollahs, from the Crusaders to the Zionists, from the Byzantines to the modern Imperialists. It is not likely to change in days ahead, regardless of how fervent our detante.

of HENRY KISSINGER (1923–) ȷo

Jerusalem, great hymn of the ages, provocation to bitter wars, and aspiration of longing hearts, thou art a puzzle of an eternal and metaphysical import.

᳊ JAMES AMOS BALDWIN (1669–1711) ᳊

No empire can ever be wrought without the peace of Jerusalem at its center because that is the hinge of history. But then, no empire can ever be wrought with the peace of Jerusalem at its center because such peace is humanly unattainable. It is an impossible mysterious mistress.

᳊ NAPOLEON BONAPARTE (1769–1821) ᳊

Now in the hands of the Mullahs and Talabehs, these symbols of our great heritage shall give new impetus to the export of our revolution. Soon the spirit of Allah will sweep the faithful Umma of the Persian hoards across the earth: first, Jerusalem will be liberated for prayer; then, the Great Satan will be humiliated and crushed; and finally, our Ji'had will free the oppressed masses on every continent.

᳊ AYATOLLAH RUHOLLAH KHOMEINI (1900–1989) ᳊

From the confines of Jerusalem a horrible tale has gone forth. An accursed race, a race utterly alienated from God, has invaded the lands of those Christians and depopulated them by the sword, plundering, and fire. Recall therefore the greatness of Charlemagne. O most valiant soldiers, descendents of invincible ancestors, be not degenerate. Let all hatred between you depart, all quarrels end, all wars cease. Start upon the road to the Holy Sepulcher, to tear that land from a wicked race and subject it to yourselves thereby restoring it to Christ. I call you to take the cross and redeem defiled Jerusalem. *Deus vult.*

POPE URBAN II (1035–1099)

Be assured that the many indignities heaped upon the Palestinian people since ancient times must and shall be avenged. Israel's policy in the occupied territories is little more than an extension of the imperialist tactics of the conqueror Joshua. Surely the judgment of Allah is reserved for them until Jerusalem is transferred from Dar al Harb to Dar al Islam. Ishamael shall have his revenge.

YASSER ARAFAT (1929–)

To emerge from the architectural and acoustical marvels within the Church of Saint Anne, built by the Crusaders just adjacent to the five porticoes of the Pool of Bethesda, only to be confronted with uzi-bearing soldiers is indeed discomfiting and disorienting. To pray in the Church of the Holy Sepulchre before Golgotha under the watchful eyes of security police with walkie-talkies is likewise a strange anomaly. To wander down the Via Dolorosa recalling the chronology of the Gospel accounts of the passion of Jesus Christ, with the angry anarchy of the Saracen Quarter as a backdrop, is surely misbegotten. But then, that is Jerusalem as much as the glorious view from the Mount of Olives or the dust swirling through the crowded streets along the Kidron Valley, as much as the quietude of Gordon's Garden Tomb or the frenzied bustle around the Damascus Gate, as much as the intensity of Shabat or the solemnity of Ramadan.

ᴏᶩ TRISTAN GYLBERD (1954–) ᶩᴏ

Pray for the peace of Jerusalem.

ᴏᶩ PSALM 122 ᶩᴏ

Mark Twain in 1867

Abraham was known as a man of faith. But it is the fruit of his doubt that has most shaped the spiritual and geo-political crisis in the Middle East—and particularly in the central city of the Middle East, Jerusalem.

God promised him an heir. When he came up out of Ur in the land of the Chaldees, God told him that through that heir, the nations would be blessed. Through that heir, a mighty people would be raised up that would be the focal point of faith, hope, and love the world over. Abraham believed, and thus became the "friend of God."

But that promised heir was not forthcoming. Years passed, then decades. As time slowly wore on, Abraham began to have subtle doubts. He began to fear that he had perhaps misunderstood God's promise. Sarah, his wife, was barren, and they were both becoming quite elderly. The possibility of a natural heir seemed impossible. So he and Sarah decided to take matters into their own hands.

And that was when the troubles really began.

In some parts of the ancient Middle East, it was obligatory for a barren wife to provide her husband with an indentured concubine who would bear children for her by proxy. Legally, the children were to be the issue of the wife, not the servant. In their doubt, Abraham and Sarah resorted to this surrogacy scheme, and a child was thus conceived. They named him Ishmael.

Fourteen years later, they saw how foolish they had been ever to doubt God's promise. A child was born to Sarah. The natural child they had yearned for was theirs. They named him Isaac.

Conflict between these two sons of Abraham began almost from the start. One was born according to the flesh, the other was born according to the spirit. The one, disinherited by the other, apparently became bitter, mocking and persecuting his half brother. Eventually, the situation became so intolerable that Sarah demanded that Ishmael and his Egyptian concubine mother, Hagar, be expelled from the family to wander in the desert.

Alas, that was hardly the end of the matter. Indeed, it was barely the beginning.

According to Christian and Jewish traditions, Ishmael went to live in the wilderness of Paran, in the region of Hejaz. There he had twelve patriarchal sons, as did both of his nephews, Jacob and Esau. The Bible associates the clans and tribes descended from him with the Midianites, the Edomites, the Egyptians, and the Assyrians. Interestingly, this concurs with Islamic tradition, which asserts that Ishmael settled in the city of Mecca, which eventually became the capital of Hejaz and the holy city of Islam. There he became the unquestioned leader of all the diverse desert peoples throughout the Middle East.

Meanwhile, Isaac begat a long line of faithful men—Jacob, Joseph, Moses, Joshua, Gideon, and David—who were able to claim the full inheritance of Abraham: the land of Israel and the city of Jerusalem.

From Isaac came the Jews.

From Ishmael came the Arabs.

And the two have been at enmity with one another ever since.

Thus, the doubt of Abraham has borne bitter fruit.

Interestingly, it was William Blake who first gave the name Jerusalem to all that was tender and lovely in the human soul. He wrote of her as a beautiful woman who maintains her virtue despite the indignities imposed by the ages. He described her as a pristine kingdom whose true spirit has fallen asleep but will not die, despite the decline of man and his ignominious fall. Blake's poetic instinct grasped the truth that this city, perhaps more than any other, has always paradoxically and paradigmatically nourished both sincere holiness and sincere betrayal—from as long ago as the doubt of Abraham.

In Jerusalem, the present is but a gossamer above ages past. History is inescapable. It hangs in the air like the wail of the faithful before the Western Wall. It intrudes on every conversation like the wheedling cries of the Arab merchants at the Jaffa Gate. It pierces every waking moment like the glinting gold of the Haram es Sherif against the Judean sky. And yet the gossamer is thick and dull.

That was what most impressed Mark Twain when he visited the city in 1867 as a part of the "first organized pleasure party ever assembled for a transatlantic voyage." It was a Grand Tour for the rich and famous of America, who weary of war and reconstruction at home, set out to see the sights in Europe and beyond.

Twain was not yet able to assume the pose of a laureate ex-officio—he had only published a few newspaper articles, editorials, humor pieces, and a single book of frontier-style short stories. All of his great work—and the fame and fortune that would accompany it—still lay ahead of him. Nevertheless, his quick wit, his ready criticism, and his unerring eye lent the trip remarkable clarity and vision.

Everywhere he looked in Jerusalem, he saw the paradox of Abraham's doubt and the evidence of its bitter fruit. As yet, Zionism had not brought waves of Jewish immigrants to the city from Europe. And there were hardly any Palestinian Moslems in the city either. Instead, the largest part of the meager population was comprised of Christians. Some were the native remnant of the old Byzantine culture. Others were pilgrims who found their soul's rest in the city of their Lord's passion. Thus, as it had been for a great part of its existence through the ages, Jerusalem was a Christian city, dominated by Christian concerns.

The Ottoman Turks, who ruled over the region at the time, had allowed the little town to fall into a shameful state of disrepair. As a result, the Christians, along with the tiny community of Hasidic Jews who lived there, were the caretakers of its glorious spiritual, historical, and cultural heritage. Yet, apart from a few crumbling relics there was hardly any visible evidence of that heritage to be found anywhere. Twain had to wonder what there was in the city actually worth fighting over.

Despite the presence of the Church of the Holy Sepulchre, the Al Aqusa Mosque, the meandering Via Dolorosa, and the walls of Sulieman the Magnificent, Jerusalem seemed to be utterly devoid of interesting sites to visit. There were no great museums as there had been in all the other cities of the Grand Tour. There were no marvels of architectural wonder. There were no great paintings to admire, no remarkable statues to appreciate, and no public spaces to amble about. Instead, Jerusalem was like the Holy of Holies in the old Temple of Solomon: strangely, profoundly empty, yet mystically, powerfully plenteous.

Unlike in London or Paris or Rome, the attractions of Jerusalem were less tangible, and yet more substantial. They were less visible, yet more evident.

Though he remained rather skeptical, his visit to the city clearly affected Twain. The themes of history and spirituality he encountered there would continue to dominate his writing long after he returned home. He recorded his thoughts in the breakthrough book, *Innocents Abroad.* But even then he was not finished with them. Indeed, they would haunt his writing ever afterward as is evident in such books as *Huckleberry Finn, Connecticut Yankee in King Arthur's Court, Joan of Arc, The Prince and the Pauper,* and *Tom Sawyer Abroad.*

The impress of Jerusalem, the city of eternal hope in the midst of temporal strife, was to leave an indelible mark upon Twain's life— just as it has on so many other lives before and since.

A PALESTINIAN BANQUET

*The tribes and tongues of all the world being well represented in
Jerusalem offer a wild diversion for the palate.*

MARK TWAIN (1835–1910)

Falafel

*2 c cooked chick peas, ½ c water, 1 T flour, 1 egg, 4 oz. crumbled bread,
4 cloves minced garlic, ¼ t each: cumin, basil, marjoram, salt to taste, flour
for dredging, fat for deep frying, 4 T chopped mint*

Mash chick peas until a coarse paste results. In a bowl combine
the peas with water, flour, egg, bread, and garlic. Add spices and salt
to taste. Form into small balls and dredge in flour. Fry in a skillet in
very hot fat until deep brown. Drain. Sprinkle with mint and serve
with flatbread.

Eggplant

*1 eggplant, 1 T salt, ¼ c olive oil, 3 cloves minced garlic, 1 c yogurt,
2 T chopped mint*

Slice eggplant. Sprinkle with salt, cover lightly, and let stand for
10 minutes. Saute eggplant slices in olive oil. Drain and cool. In a
bowl combine garlic, yogurt, and mint. Pour yogurt sauce over eggplant and serve.

Challah

2 c warm water, 1 T sugar, ¼ t powdered saffron, ¼ c olive oil, about 4 T dry yeast, 6 c flour, 2 beaten eggs, 1 T salt

In a bowl add sugar, saffron, and oil to warm water. Add yeast and 1 c flour to mixture. Let rise for 30 minutes. Stir eggs in, alternating with remaining flour. Add salt, stirring well. Turn onto floured board and knead well for 10 minutes or until dough is elastic and glossy. Cover with warm floured cloth and let rise until doubled, about 1½ hours. Knead again, then cut in half. Cut each half into 3 pieces and roll these to make long rolls. Braid rolls together, turning under at ends to make oval loaves. Place on a baking sheet and let rise 30 minutes longer. Brush with egg yolk and water mixture. Bake in a hot oven for about 45 minutes or until golden brown.

Gefilte Fish

3 lbs. assorted fish, 4 medium chopped onions, 2 eggs, ¼ c cold water, 2–3 T matzo meal, 2 t salt, 1 t white pepper, 1 t sugar, fish trimmings and roe (if available), 2 sliced carrots, 2 sliced stalks celery

Cut fish into fillets, but keep trimmings and roe. Salt lightly and place in refrigerator for several hours. Pat dry. Chop fish coarsely. Add 2 onions to fish. Chop and work in eggs, water, and enough matzo meal to have the consistency of thick oatmeal. Add salt, pepper, and sugar. Place trimmings, remaining 2 onions, carrots, and celery in a soup pot. Add water just to cover and bring to a boil. Shape fish mixture into balls and drop gently into boiling broth. Simmer for about 1 hour. Add water to keep covered, if needed. Cool for about 30 minutes. Remove fish balls and vegetables to a deep bowl, and strain broth over. Chill overnight.

Tabbouleh

1 c bulghur wheat, 3 c chopped parsley, ¼ c chopped mint leaves, 5 minced green onions, 3 chopped tomatoes, juice of 2 lemons, ½ c olive oil, salt to taste

Soak bulghur in warm water to cover for 1 hour. Drain and squeeze out as much water as possible. Combine with parsley, mint, green onions, tomatoes, lemon juice, olive oil, and salt to taste. Chill and serve.

Assorted Fresh Fruit

Rome

In the final analysis, Paris belongs to Parisians, and London to Londoners, but Rome belongs to the world. Rome's almost gravitational pull has attracted, in addition to travelers, some of the most creative artists and thinkers of every era. All that surrounds a visitor in Rome—the stunning art and architecture, the terrible traffic, the grandeur of scale and even the lively, almost hyperanimated, citizens—guarantees an unforgettable visit. If you had only one hour in the city and visited St. Peter's, or admired the panorama from the top of the Spanish Steps at sunset, or walked around the Colosseum to catch a glimpse of the Forum from the gates, you'd well understand why Rome is called the Eternal City. Since the earliest days of travel visitors have found their way there—an astonishing city influenced equally by the empires of antiquity, the aspirations of the Renaissance, and the inclinations of Modernity—for in truth, all roads lead to Rome.

Rome! The city of all time and of all the world.
> ❦ NATHANIEL HAWTHORNE (1804–1864) ❧

O Rome! My country! City of the soul!
> ❦ LORD BYRON (1788–1824) ❧

I've stood on Achilles' tomb
And heard Troy doubted:
Time will doubt of Rome.
> ❦ LORD BYRON (1788–1824) ❧

Ah, the glory that was Greece,
And the grandeur that was Rome.
> ❦ EDGAR ALLAN POE (1809–1849) ❧

In Rome—in the Forum—there opened one night
A gulf. All the augurs turned pale at the sight.
In this omen the anger of Heaven they read.
Men consulted the gods: then the oracle said:
Ever open this gulf shall endure, till at last
That which Rome hath most precious within it will be cast.
The Romans threw in their corn and their stuff,
But the gulf yawned as wide. Rome seemed likely enough
To be ruined ere this rent in her heart she could choke.
Then curtius reveing the oracle spoke:
O Quirites, to this Heaven's question has come:
What to Rome is most precious? The manhood of Rome.
He plunged, and the gulf closed.

         EARL OF LYTTON (1831–1891)

Rome will eternally be the eternal city.

         WILLIAM MAKEPEACE THACKERAY (1811–1863)

We are all sons and daughters of the Roman civilization, the Roman triumph, the Roman vision. Its whole vast vocabulary—of art, music, literature, architecture, sculpture, and ideas—is woven into our very souls.

         JOHN RUSKIN (1819–1900)

Every town worth talking about has a shape; only the great unorganized town-planned modern city is not worth talking about; and nobody as a matter of fact ever does talk about it, in the sense in which men will never leave off talking about Rome. Everybody knows that the precipitous terraces of Edinburgh are like the profile of a particular human face. Everybody who thinks of Bath thinks of the particular way in which particular gray crescents of houses lie on particular green crescents of hills. There are aspects in which Paris seems almost to stand in the Seine as much as Venice in the sea; it is really the Island of the City; and Notre Dame looks taller than the mere Eiffel Tower. And so it is with Rome. The heart of Rome is not to be seen in the sites or sights—as if such a place could be sight-seen—but there is a particularity which is very much worth talking about. So much so, indeed, has this conversation consumed the minds and imaginations of men that after some two millennia they are still engaged in it.

ᛝ G. K. CHESTERTON (1874–1936) ᛞ

While stands the Coliseum, Rome shall stand;
When falls the Coliseum, Rome shall fall;
And when Rome falls—the world.

ᛝ LORD BYRON (1788–1824) ᛞ

The hand that rounded Peter's dome,
And groiuned the aisles of Christian Rome,
Wrought in a sad sincerity;
Himself from God he could not free,
He builded better than he knew;
The conscious stone to beauty grew.

ᴥ RALPH WALDO EMERSON (1803–1882) ᴥ

Quando hic sum, non jejuno Sabbato; quando Romae sum, jejuno Sabbato.
When in Rome, do as the Romans do.

ᴥ ST. AMBROSE (339–397) ᴥ

For my part, I had rather be the first man among these fellows, than the second man in Rome.

ᴥ JULIUS CAESAR (101–44 BC) ᴥ

In these boots and with this staff
Two hundred leagues and a half
Walked I, went I, paced I, tripped I,
Marched I, held I, skelped I, slipped I,
Pushed I, panted, swung, and dashed I,
Picked I, forded, swam, and splashed I,
Strolled I, climbed I, crawled and scrambled,
Dropped and dipped I, ranged and rambled;
Plodded I, hobbled I, trudged and tramped I,
And in lonely spinnies, camped I,
And in haunted pinewoods slept I,
Lingered, loitered, limped, and crept I,
Clambered, halted, stepped, and leapt I,
Slowly sauntered, roundly strode I, And:

Oh! Patron saints and Angels
That protect the four Evangels!
And you prophets vel majores
Vel incerti, vel minores,
Virgines ac confessores
Chief of whose peculiar glories
Est in Aula Regis stare
Atque orare et exorare
Et clamare et conclamare
Clamantes cum clamoribus
Pro Nobis Peccatoribus.

Let me not conceal it: rode I.
For who but critics could complain
Of riding in a railway train?
Across the valleys and the highland
With all the world on either hand
Drinking when I had a mind to,
Singing when I felt inclined to;
Never turned my face to home
Till I had slaked my heart at Rome.

                 ❧ HILAIRE BELLOC (1870–1953) ❧

Island of saints, still constant, still allied
To the great truths opposed to human pride;
Island of ruins, towers, cloisters grey,
Whence palmer kings with pontiffs once did stray
To Rome and Sion, or to kindle fire
Which amid the darkness can inspire
Lands that in fondest memory and song
Thy pristine glory fearlessly prolong.
>> KENELIN HENRY DIGBY (1800–1880) <<

Rome is the mother country of us all—it is the great progenitor.
>> EUGENE LEE HAMILTON (1845–1907) <<

I fail to see how any man—be he Catholic, Protestant, Heathen, or
some indefinite sojourner in the nether realms of the Modernist
Indecision—be not moved at the sites and sights of Christendom's
glorious genesis.
>> TRISTAN GYLBERD (1954–) <<

Hilaire Belloc in 1901

By the time Hilaire Belloc visited Rome in 1901—after a long journey on foot from France, across the Alps, and through Lombardy—it was universally recognized as one of the grandest cities in the world. Tens of thousands of pilgrims and tourists came to admire, and be awed by, its treasures of architecture, art, and history every year. It was a well worn cliché that all roads led to Rome.

But such had not always been the case. Indeed, by the fourteenth century, the great ancient city had dwindled to a miserable village. Perhaps 20,000 people clung to the ruins of the old Roman Empire and the early center of Christendom despite the ravages of disease and robber barons. Popes and cardinals had fled to the comfort and safety of Avignon in southern France. And to make matters worse, even in Italy, Rome was dwarfed in wealth and power by the great commercial cities and territorial states farther north, from Florence to Venice. The city had become a pitiful shadow of its once glorious former self.

But during the Renaissance, the See of Saint Peter returned to the ancient, crumbling city. And a dramatic course of rehabilitation was begun that would last for several centuries. Popes and cardinals straightened streets, raised bridges across the Tiber, provided hospitals, fountains, and new churches for the public and splendid palaces and gardens for themselves. They drew on all the riches of

Renaissance art and architecture to adorn the urban fabric, which they saw as tangible proof of the power and glory of the church. And they attracted pilgrims from all of Christian Europe, whose alms and living expenses made the city rich once more. The papal curia—the central administration of the church—became one of the most efficient governments in Europe. Michelangelo and Raphael, Castiglione and Cellini, Giuliano da Sangallo and Domenico Fontana all lived and worked in Rome. Architecture, painting, music, and literature flourished.

Much of the reason for such a Herculean effort to revive the city was simply that during the Renaissance, Italian intellectuals had become increasingly fascinated by the physical as well as the literary relics of the ancient world. Indeed, despite its many advances in art, music, medicine, science, and technology, the Renaissance was essentially a nostalgic revival of ancient pagan ideals and values. The dominating ideas were those of classical humanism, pregnable naturalism, and antinomian individualism—or in other words the magnificent materialism and ribald hedonism of the past. Taking their cues primarily from ancient Greece and Rome, the leaders of the epoch were not so much interested in the Christian notion of progress as they were in the heathen ideal of innocence. Reacting to the artificialities and contrivances of the medieval period, they dispatched the Christian consensus it had wrought with enervating aplomb.

Throughout history, men have reacted instead of acted in times of crisis. They have sought to ameliorate an ill on the right hand by turning immediately and entirely to the left. They have tried to solve a problem in the crumbling citadels of the immediate by unearthing the broken foundations of an even more distant past. Driven by extremism, they have failed to see the moderating application of adjustments and alternatives.

When faced with the recalcitrance of feudal life, the immediate reaction of the people of the Renaissance was to reject out of hand the very foundations of their Christian heritage—often even in the name of Christian advance—instead of actually building on that heritage for the future.

No society can long stand without some ruling set of principles, some overriding values, or some ethical standard. Thus, when the men and women of the fourteenth through the nineteenth centuries threw off Christian mores, they necessarily went casting about for a suitable alternative. And so, Greek and Roman thought was exhumed from the ancient sarcophagus of paganism. Aristotle, Plato, and Pythagoras were dusted off, dressed up, and rehabilitated as the newly tenured voices of wisdom. Cicero, Seneca, and Herodotus were raised from the philosophical crypt and made to march to the tune of a new era.

Every forum, every arena, and every aspect of life began to reflect this newfound fascination with the pre-Christian past. Art, architecture, music, drama, literature, and every other form of popular culture began to portray the themes of classical humanism, pregnable naturalism, and antinomian individualism.

Ironically then, ancient Rome therefore became a very tangible symbol for the future. The exhumation of its ruins became part and parcel with the exhumation of the pagan idealism upon which the Renaissance would be founded.

And of course, Rome had the grand ruins to exhume—ruins at which medieval pilgrims had long marveled. The Roman in the street was happy to provide misinformation about sites and statues, but in the Renaissance, scholars began to measure, excavate, and identify the statues and buildings that had long amazed travelers. Of course, much was lost forever. When Poggio Bracciolini and a friend climbed the Capitoline Hill in 1430, the vast view that opened out before them was a desert; the ancient forum was populated only by pigs, deer, and vegetables. But by the end of the fifteenth century, Roman scholars had identified the sites of many lost buildings, compiled notebooks bulging with information, and begun to recreate the ancient city.

Between 1450 and 1600, ancient Rome began to emerge from beneath the shapeless pastures and deserted hills of the ancient city. Renaissance scholars identified major sites and buildings. They began the great effort of copying the ancient inscriptions that made the city itself a vast, if fragmentary, textbook about Roman history and life.

By the middle of the fifteenth century, scholars in the curia—like the brilliant architect Leon Battista Alberti and the erudite scholar Flavio Biondo—knew the ancient city better than anyone had for a thousand years. Artists recorded the ruins that survived, broken and ivy-covered, and reconstructed the original palaces and temples in all their crisp-edged glory. Architects tried to grasp the rules and methods of the Roman builders. When ancient works of art, like the Laocoon, came to light they immediately became famous and influential, finding prominent places in the sculpture collections that adorned the Capitoline hill, the Belvedere court of the Vatican, and many private houses. Drawn and printed images of them circulated throughout Europe and scholars and artists made pilgrimages to Rome to see them.

By the middle of the sixteenth century, Roman scholars had recreated the whole web and texture of ancient Roman life, from its physical environment to its religious rituals, in astonishingly vivid detail. True, not even papal support could stop the destruction of individual monuments and buildings; much continued to be lost or scattered. The study of the ruins prospered even as buildings were torn down or burned to make lime. In the course of the seventeenth and eighteenth centuries, Roman archaeologists shed new light on the Egyptian and early Christian worlds as well as on Rome itself.

The new buildings that they built—the churches, the monuments, the palaces, the public works, and the commercial edifices—were thus greatly influenced by the legacy of antiquity. The ancient world was essentially resurrected in the new. This was the odd cultural juxtaposition that Hilaire Belloc encountered as he made his way into the eternal city in 1901.

Belloc was born outside Paris in 1870. Two years later, his father, a French citizen, died, so his mother removed the youngster and his sister to her native England where they would be raised. He was trained in the finest schools in the land and quickly gained renown as a fine poet, an incisive historian, and an essayist of great promise. An ardent Catholic and proud of his dual citizenship and heritage, he maintained close ties to his father's family in France and upheld his responsibilities to serve in the French armed services. It was following one of his tours of duty there that he impetuously decided to walk all the way to Rome as a kind of modern-day pilgrimage. He wanted to find the roots of his faith—and to discover the sites and sights of Christendom's genesis.

That he did and more. The story of his remarkable journey was recorded in his classic book, *The Path to Rome.* But the insights he gained and the perspective that he solidified also pervaded his more than one hundred books that followed in his long and accomplished career as an historian, apologist, controversialist, politician, economic theorist, novelist, poet, journalist, and pundit.

It was there, amidst the unearthed splendors of the pagan Antiquity and the rebuilt glories of the pagan Renaissance, that he found the genius of Western Civilization, its ultimate continuity, and its conflict with the Reformation—themes that would shape his social criticism and define his curmudgeonly prophecies against the advancing horrors of modernity. In essence, it was his trip to Rome that made him so interesting and so infuriating.

A Roman Meal

The brilliance of Christendom may be savored as well at a fine Roman meal as at a fine Roman shrine.

Hilaire Belloc (1870–1953)

Guinea Hen Stuffed with Goose Liver

4 oz. goose liver mixed with 1 T white wine, 1 T butter, 8 oz. bread-crumbs, 1/2 c milk, 1 beaten egg, 1/4 t dried thyme, 1/4 t dried sage, 1 T Cognac, salt and pepper to taste, 2 guinea hens, 1 c dry white wine, 4 c chicken broth, 1 onion, 2 sliced carrots, 1 bay leaf, 6 juniper berries, 1 t peppercorns

Cream the goose liver and wine with softened butter. Moisten the breadcrumbs with milk and egg, and add to the liver. Season with thyme, sage, Cognac, salt, and pepper. Stuff hens with liver mixture. Place in a heavy pot with wine, chicken broth, quartered onion, carrots, bay leaf, berries, and peppercorns. Bring to a boil and simmer, covered, for 1 hour. Remove birds and serve.

Vitello Roma

4 oz. anchovy fillets, 2 cloves minced garlic, 4 lb. leg of boned veal (skinned and tied into a roll), 1 large onion (quartered), 1 bay leaf, 2 T chopped parsley, 8 oz. tuna, 1 c olive oil, juice of 1 lemon, 4 T capers, salt and pepper, lemon slices

Chop one anchovy fine and add to minced garlic. Make several incisions in veal and put anchovy mixture in each. Place in deep pot, and add onion, bay leaf, parsley, and boiling water to cover. Simmer for about 2 hours. Remove meat from broth and chill. Strain broth and reserve. Pound tuna almost to a paste, adding the rest of the anchovies and the olive oil, lemon juice, and capers. Add reserved broth if needed to thin sauce. Season with salt and pepper to taste. Cut veal into thin slices and arrange on serving platter. Pour sauce over the meat and top with lemon slices.

Gnocchi Di Patate

6 baking potatoes, 3 egg yolks, 2 t salt, 2 c flour, melted butter, grated cheese

Bake potatoes until tender. Peel, mash, and chill overnight. Mix the potatoes with egg yolks and salt. Turn the mixture onto a lightly floured board. Make a well in the center and add flour in small increments, kneading and adding only as much as needed, until dough is smooth and no longer sticky. Do not let it become dry and crumbly. Roll dough into long rolls about 1-inch wide. Slice into 1-inch pieces. Press finger in middle of each slice so that dough will curl toward center.

Bring 3 quarts salted water to a boil and add gnocchi. Reduce heat and cook uncovered until gnocchi float to the surface; cook about 5 minutes more. Remove and serve with melted butter and grated cheese.

Broccoli Romani

1 bunch broccoli, salt, 4 T butter, 2 T olive oil, 2 cloves garlic, ½ c bread-crumbs

Wash the broccoli and remove woody parts of stems. Boil in salted water for 10 minutes. Drain and set aside. Heat butter and 1 T olive oil and sauté garlic. Add remaining butter and breadcrumbs, then sprinkle over broccoli.

Assorted Raw Vegetables and Cheeses